Bristol City Greats

love
Rob & Bec x
2009.

Bristol City
Greats

Ivan Ponting

Tom Morgan

redcliffe

In association with the

EVENING POST

Statistical Note

The main dates accompanying the profiles refer to the seasons in which each player appeared in the City first team, not when he joined and left the club. In the brief statistical resumé at the end of each profile, goals and appearances under the heading 'Others' are in respect of matches in the Football League promotion play-offs, Welsh Cup, Football League Trophy, Watney Cup, Anglo-Scottish Cup, Anglo-Italian Cup, Associate Members' Cup, Freight Rover Trophy, Sherpa Van Trophy, Leyland Daf Cup, Zenith Data Systems Cup, Auto Windscreens Shield and LDV Vans Trophy. The figures under the heading 'Other Clubs' includes League appearances and goals only. Substitute appearances are in brackets. Figures relating to the League Cup also refer to its successors, the Milk Cup, Littlewoods Cup, Rumbelows Cup, Coca-Cola Cup, Worthington Cup and Carling Cup. Figures in the 'On The Bench' section which begins on page 150 refer to all first-class games for the club. All records are complete to the end of the 2004/05 season.

First published by Redcliffe Press Ltd., in 1990
This new and enlarged edition published in 2005 by Redcliffe Press Ltd., 81g Pembroke Road, Bristol BS8 3EA

© Ivan Ponting and Tom Morgan

ISBN 1 904537 33 2

British Library Cataloguing-in-Publication Data
A catalogue record for this book is available from the British Library

DESIGNED BY STEPHEN MORRIS COMMUNICATIONS, SMC@FREEUK.COM
PRINTED AND BOUND IN MALTA BY GUTENBERG PRESS LTD

Contents

Introduction

THE LATE JOHN ATYEO was not just a marvellous centre-forward with a god-given knack of scoring goals; he was a footballing romantic, too, blessed with a fertile imagination, and a vision of how Bristol City had the scope to grow.

Only a week or two before his sudden, shockingly premature death, he gazed across Ashton Gate, sighed deeply and declared: 'This club could be the Manchester United of the West Country. The opportunity is there and all we have to do is seize it. The potential fan-base is colossal, but we've got to give the people something they can really believe in. There's a special aura about this place, so much has happened here down the years — and it's dripping with a magic that is still untapped.'

As he continued to muse on his field of dreams, I found myself empathising unreservedly with John. His wistful train of thought took me back to the far-off days of my boyhood, when impromptu football games in the field next to the family farmhouse were deadly serious affairs, and every young player would take on the character of a sporting hero as we lived out our fantasies. I was usually Bobby Charlton or Tommy Taylor; occasionally I might even stretch to Alfredo di Stefano, the incomparable centre-piece of Real Madrid.

But after I was taken in hand by Melv and Jeff Ford, a pair of sports-mad brothers who lived just down the road in my home village of Chewton Mendip, there were suddenly new idols to emulate. Melv took me along to Ashton Gate, Jeff to Eastville, and henceforth the names of Atyeo and Rovers' Alfie Biggs took their places of honour in the cup finals among the cow-pats.

Duly I became a regular follower of both Bristol clubs, and in the first edition of this book, which was published in 1990, I attempted to recall, in words and pictures, the men who gave me so much entertainment over the years, as well as some of the most accomplished Robins of the immediate post-war period.

When an update was mooted for 2005, to embrace newer luminaries such as Jackie Dziekanowski and, more recently, the exciting Leroy Lita, it seemed like an appropriate notion. The trouble was that circumstances had curtailed my attendance record at Ashton Gate over the last decade and a half, so I didn't feel qualified for the job.

Happily, I knew a fellow who was, the talented young writer Tom Morgan, who covers City professionally, so we joined forces to produce this volume.

To back our own observations we have talked to players from various eras who, without exception, have offered enthusiastic assistance. Last time I was limited by reasons of space to profiles of 50 post-war Robins; this time we have added 20 more, though opinions might differ radically about some of our selections. However, arguing about football is almost as enjoyable as watching it, and if we have managed to stimulate some spirited debate, we shall be delighted.

Those whose favourites have been passed over may be slightly mollified by the section at the back, which contains photographs of 48 players who just missed out, though since even that inevitably omits many much-loved performers, probably we shan't get off the hook so easily.

In the first edition I wrote that life is never dull for those who follow Bristol City, and nothing has changed. True, there have been some dashed hopes in the 21st century but, who knows, with Brian Tinnion at the helm, maybe the Robins will make significant progress towards John Atyeo's seductive idyll.

Here's hoping, because if one day we get round to a third edition of *Bristol City Greats*, maybe after the 2019/2020 season, it would mean that there'll be no shortage of new stars to fire the imagination.

Ivan Ponting, September 2005

Acknowledgements

FROM IVAN PONTING
Pat, Rosie and Joe Ponting for unending patience and support; Stephen Morris for revolutionising the design; Clara Sansom for enlightened editorship; Andy Cowie of Colorsport for never being beaten; Chris Marsh and Dudley D, commitment personified; Chris Bartlett, John England and Rob Stokes of the *Evening Post*; Peter Spiring; John Sansom.

FROM TOM MORGAN
Brian Tinnion; Gerry Sweeney; Tony Fawthrop; Shaun Taylor; David Foot. Special thanks to my mother Quita, my journalistic heroine.

FURTHER ACKNOWLEDGEMENTS FROM THE FIRST BOOK
John Atyeo; Doug Baker; George Baker; Les Bardsley; Bob Boyd; Alec Briggs; Tony Cook; Keith Fear; Melv Ford; Mike Gibson; Peter Godsiff; Lucy Graham; John Hudson; Bobby Jones; Richard Latham; Gordon Parr; Arnold Rodgers; Jimmy Rogers; John Sansom; Alan Skirton; Steve Small; Ken Wimshurst; Gerry Brooke and the staff of the *Evening Post* library; all at Colorsport.

Foreword

WHY DOESN'T A CITY THE SIZE OF BRISTOL HAVE A PREMIERSHIP FOOTBALL CLUB? I have had that conversation with local people so many times it seems like a broken record. In truth, I don't think anyone really knows. There is a ridiculous presumption outside the West Country that Bristolians don't really care about their football. But that's wrong.

I was brought up playing for Newcastle United and I can say first-hand that fans of Bristol City are as passionate as any I have met, on Tyneside or anywhere else. Football is taken very seriously around here. Since I arrived in 1993 I have never been to a restaurant, or even to a supermarket, without someone coming over to talk about our progress. Bristol City has become part of me. I live near the ground, and I think I always will. It's an institution with a huge fan-base and an amazing history; it deserves and it demands the very best.

The club cherishes its cult heroes. Atyeo, Garland, Merrick, Dziekanowski. . . the list goes on and on. Indeed, since those illustrious names forged their glorious niches in Ashton Gate folklore there have been dozens of other magnificent talents, alongside whom I have been privileged to play during my dozen seasons as a Robin. This book, Bristol City Greats, fulfils a crucial function in recapturing and preserving the memories of all those marvellous footballers.

When I find time for a moment of reflection, it seems unreal that I have been at the club for so long, but the days have flown by. I must admit to suffering a pang when finally I hung up my boots at the end of last season, but although I'm watching from the sidelines now, I can tell the supporters that, in my mind, I am kicking every ball with each one of them. Some were surprised when I took on the manager's job but I am not using it as a stepping stone to move on to a bigger club. I want to make Bristol City a top club for the long term. I am fortunate enough to have played more than 500 games here and I want to repay everyone involved by getting them back to where they deserve to be.

I am sure we are heading in the right direction. Investment in the academy has been extremely valuable, and this club has an exciting future. Now we must take responsibility to ensure that we grasp our opportunity. I am confident that we shall and I am ready to predict that, over the next few years, there will be plenty of additions to the collection of heroes featured between these covers. I feel genuinely that Bristol City will not be waiting long to reach the Promised Land.

Brian Tinnion, Ashton Gate 2005

BORN: Adelaide, Australia, 9.6.75

CITY RECORD:

League: 63 (21) games, 19 goals

FA Cup: 4 games, 5 goals

League Cup: 6 (2) games, 2 goals

Others: 4 (2) games, 0 goals

Total: 77 (25) games, 26 goals

OTHER CLUBS:

Young Boys of Berne, Switzerland

Munich 1860, Germany

Australia caps

PAUL AGOSTINO

1995/96 — 1996/97

PAUL AGOSTINO was good for ticket sales, particularly among Bristol's female population. The Aussie striker looked like a tanned surf dude who had just stepped off the famous white sands at Bondi Beach. He proved a major hit with the ladies during his years in Bristol, but also he melted the hearts of the Ashton Gate faithful, not least for his role in turning around the Bristol Rovers derby hoodoo.

As a 16-year-old, the striker had revealed mercurial talent in helping his country to reach the semi-finals of the World Youth Cup, and shrewd observers marked him out for glory at the highest level. But when he arrived in England for trials with several League clubs, it was only City coaches Joe Jordan and Tony Fawthrop who dared to pay the £50,000 needed to prise him away from the Swiss side Young Boys of Berne.

As it turned out, the Robins had provided the launchpad for a potentially glittering career. Not too long after Agostino's departure in the summer of 1997 to seek fame and fortune in the German top flight with Munich 1860, his new employers received an enquiry about his availability from AC Milan, who withdrew only after being reportedly quoted a price-tag of £18 million. That is an amazing turnaround for a guy who had been surprised when City had offered him his initial deal.

Though he hailed from Down Under, it didn't take the newcomer long to acquire a taste for Bristol derby action. During the early 1990s,

undoubtedly the blue half of the city enjoyed the better of those passionate encounters, but plucky Paul turned the tide. During his two years at the club the Robins never lost a showdown with Rovers, the Adelaide-born star finding the net in three of his four derbies, including a mesmerising solo effort at Ashton Gate in December 1996, regrettably shunted from the headlines by a pitch invasion.

The Agostino scoring rate was never remarkable but he always brought more to the team than mere goals. Paul's natural athleticism was supplemented by enviable flair and vision, which produced rich reward for the likes of his countryman David Seal and, a little later, Shaun Goater.

Towards the end of 1996/97 his performances appeared to be improving with every game and he was rewarded with a first full international call-up. Thus his departure to Munich, shortly before his 22nd birthday, hit City like a bombshell. By then he had formed an enterprising partnership with Goater as the club narrowly missed out on promotion through the play-offs, and supporters were appalled that he had turned his back on the Robins to leave on a Bosman-style free transfer.

But the Australian had been offered £4,000-a-week, a free flat and a new car. Understandably enough, he felt it was too good to refuse. Paul Agostino always had the film-star looks, and now he would have the wallet to match.

WAYNE ALLISON

1990/91 — 1994/95

STICKS AND STONES never broke his bones and words couldn't hurt him either. Wayne Allison was an immense individual, in terms of both physique and personality. The smile never disappeared from the face of City's bulky, bustling buccaneer of a striker, even when his detractors wrote him off as a battering ram only worthy of the lower leagues. In truth, often the Yorkshireman's style was ungainly, but equally he could be deadly effective. In the heat of battle, it was criminally unwise to write off 'The Chief'.

In the 1980s at Halifax, Allison the uncut diamond was hailed as one of England's bright young talents when, as a 17-year-old rookie, he went on a prolific scoring run before he had even signed a professional contract. Watford snapped him up for £250,000 but by the time he arrived at Bristol City in 1990, in a swap deal for Mark Gavin, there were question marks hanging over his ability.

Yet despite doubts cast by Ashton Gate's elitists, who handed him the uncomplimentary tag of 'Tanglefoot', he finished as the Robins' top goal-scorer in three seasons during the early 1990s, before embarking on successful spells at Swindon, Huddersfield, Tranmere, Sheffield United and Chesterfield.

Allison's swashbuckling brand of centre-forward play never delighted the connoisseurs but certainly he was not bereft of attributes, always offering supporters value for money with his blend of power and tireless work-rate. Deservedly his popularity soared in 1993/94 as he found his best scoring form in City's memorable FA Cup run, and he was voted player of the year.

In the mouth-watering third-round clash with Liverpool, Wayne netted before the floodlights failed, and he repeated the feat the following week to force a replay at Anfield. Come that momentous Wednesday night on Merseyside, it was Wayne's flick-on that teed up Brian Tinnion's winner. Next, in the following round against Stockport, the towering spearhead plundered a hat-trick before City's hopes were finally ended by Charlton.

Wayne left the club in 1995 in a move that had as much to do with boardroom politics as with his own desire to quit Ashton Gate. Steve McMahon took him to Swindon for £500,000, a price which seemed modest at the time but which demonstrated how his reputation had soared during his five-year spell in Bristol.

He went on to play regularly in Division One, starring in rousing cup runs with both Tranmere and Sheffield United. Then, aged 34, he joined Chesterfield and crashed home a thumping header against the Robins in front of the Atyeo Stand in 2005. As his face cracked into the same old beaming grin that had lit up Ashton Gate so frequently down the years, even the most devoted of Bristol City fans might have been tempted to wish the big man well.

BORN: Huddersfield, Yorkshire, 16.10.68

CITY RECORD:

League: 149 (46) games, 48 goals

FA Cup: 12 (1) games, 5 goals

League Cup: 4 (5) games, 2 goals

Others: 6 (2) games, 3 goals

Total: 171 (54) games, 58 goals

OTHER CLUBS:

Halifax Town 86/7-88/9 (84, 23)

Watford 89/90 (7, 0)

Swindon Town 95/6-97/8 (101, 31)

Huddersfield Town 97/8-99/00 (74, 15)

Tranmere Rovers 99/00-01/02 (103, 26)

Sheffield United 02/03-03/04 (73, 7)

Chesterfield 04/05- (38, 6)

BORN: Westbury, Wiltshire, 7.2.32

DIED: Warminster, Wiltshire, 8.6.93

CITY RECORD:

League: 597 games, 315 goals

FA Cup: 42 games, 30 goals

League Cup: 6 games, 5 goals

Others: 2 games, 1 goal

Total: 647 games, 351 goals

CITY HONOURS:

Third Division South Championship 54/5

Promoted from Third Division 64/5

OTHER CLUBS:

Portsmouth (as amateur) 50/1 (1, 0)

6 England caps 1955-57

JOHN ATYEO

1951/52 — 1965/66

NEARLY 40 YEARS after his retirement, there are few who would argue with the assertion that John Atyeo was, in Bristol terms, the greatest of them all. Even Rovers fans, if caught in a mellow moment and assured that no one was listening, might just concede, with due deference to Messrs Bradford and Biggs, that Big John deserves the accolade.

Records can never tell the whole story, but in the case of the free-scoring Wiltshireman they do, for once, offer eloquent evidence. They speak of 350 goals in more than 600 games for the Robins, who built their side around him for a decade and a half, and reveal that in 12 of those 15 seasons he topped the scoring charts.

Along the way John played six times for England, scoring five goals and never finishing on the losing side; he would surely have gone on to win many more caps but for the selectors' objection to his part-time status.

There is a theory, propounded mainly by those who never saw him in his pomp, that he couldn't have been that exceptional, or he wouldn't have spent his entire career in the Second and Third Divisions. But John was a star in the days when there were still some things that money couldn't buy. Inter Milan, Arsenal and Spurs all coveted him, and in 1953/54 Liverpool came in with a £30,000 offer that would have nudged the British transfer record. That would place his value today at about £20 million, and may afford enlightenment to those who need it about his true stature.

In fact, John – a thoughtful, intelligent fellow who needed the mental stimulus of his work outside football, first as a quantity surveyor and then as a teacher – lacked nothing in his make-up as an inside-right cum centre-forward who would have thrived at any level.

He was big and strong, dominant in the air, was endowed liberally with skill and power in both feet, and possessed an acute soccer brain. With such a battery of assets, John was the target for some fearful physical punishment, but he was neither a moaner nor a seeker of retribution, and was never booked. Modest, unselfish, but single-minded in his goal quest, he was perhaps not given to chasing lost causes, but nevertheless contributed his share of honest toil.

After leaving the game, he revelled in teaching, becoming head of mathematics at a school in Warminster, where he lived with his wife and four children. He was utterly dedicated, and on exam days would rise early to offer pupils extra revision sessions at 7am – he reckoned there was more satisfaction in helping youngsters than in all his footballing glory, and right up until his sudden death he was unstinting in his time and effort.

There are men who have outstripped his total of appearances and others, though not many, who have scored more goals. But in the 117-year history of the Football League, no one has topped his awesome combination for one club. It makes you wonder what John Atyeo might have achieved if he'd taken up soccer full-time . . .

JACK BAILEY

1945/46 — 1957/58

AN UNWARY WINGER being introduced to Jack Bailey for the first time might have been excused for getting the wrong impression of the little Bristolian. Jack, mild of manner and sturdy of girth, shared a reputation with Ivor Guy as the only pair of gentlemen full-backs in the Football League. Some of his Robins team-mates even called him 'Pancho' in reference to his build, and his genial nature was hardly calculated to induce panic in even the most faint-hearted of flankmen.

In fact, Jack was a formidable opponent, courageous, strong and deceptively fleet of foot, a terrier whose footballing bite was worse than his bark. He relished a confrontation with exactly the type of forward who might have been expected to unsettle him – combative, hard-running types such as Peter McParland of Aston Villa – and his only real weakness was in the air. This mattered little as Jack enjoyed a reciprocal arrangement with lofty colleagues Dennis Roberts and the faithful Ivor; they looked after him in aerial combat, and he scooted across to cover if they were beleaguered on the ground.

Jack, a right-footed left-back, was spotted in local football by City boss Bob Hewison towards the end of the war. He soon turned professional and 12 days after making his senior debut against Cardiff City in April 1945 – in the emergency competition that replaced League football during the conflict – he returned to Ninian Park for one of the most bizarre matches in the Robins' history.

It was the second leg of a War League Cup encounter and, in an age when penalty shoot-outs were unheard of, the rules were that if aggregate scores were level at full time the game continued until a goal was scored. Thus, with the sides locked at 3-3, the contest went on . . . and on. Players were dropping with exhaustion when the Bluebirds settled the issue in the 202nd minute.

No doubt comforted by the knowledge that peacetime competitions held no such pitfalls, Jack pledged his long-term future to Ashton Gate and helped win the 1954/55 Third Division South title, although a broken arm caused him to miss half the season. He recovered to serve City for three more campaigns before joining Southern League Trowbridge in 1958.

Jack died, aged 65, soon after retiring from his job with a Bristol packaging company, and only four months after the death of his old friend and partner, Ivor Guy. For those who had known them, and for fans who recalled them in their prime, it was a moving coincidence.

BORN: Bristol, 17.6.21

DIED: Bristol, 31.12.86

CITY RECORD:

League: 348 games, 0 goals

FA Cup: 33 games, 0 goals

Total: 381 games, 0 goals

CITY HONOURS:

Third Division South Championship 54/5

BORN: Newcastle, 15.11.71

CITY RECORD:

League: 278 (16) games, 35 goals

FA Cup: 17 (1) games, 0 goals

League Cup: 16 games, 1 goal

Others: 16 (1) games, 3 goals

Total: 327 (18) games, 39 goals

CITY HONOURS:

Promotion from Second Division 97/8

LDV Vans Trophy 02/03

Auto Windscreens Shield Finalist 99/00

OTHER CLUBS:

Northampton Town 89/90-94/5 (153, 10)

Wycombe Wanderers 94/5-96/7 (118, 5)

Port Vale 05/06-

MICKEY BELL

OL' MICKEY BLUE EYES made as many come-backs as a certain late crooner of a similar description and, in the spring of 2005, the energetic thirtysomething was still ploughing a productive furrow down Bristol City's left flank.

A little more luck and a lot more credit would have been no more than Bell deserved for his worthy efforts over three-quarters of a decade at Ashton Gate. Yet after Danny Wilson shocked most observers by putting his reliable left-back on the transfer list in 2000, there was a constant stream of speculation that the Geordie was heading for the exit door.

His later years at the club were plagued with injuries and his turn of pace deserted him. But every time he was afforded a regular spell in the side, the old Mickey emerged to prove he could still be one of City's finest. No one at Ashton Gate crossed a more telling ball; his passing remained among the most accurate; and his curling free-kicks could still thrill punters and dumbfound the opposition. That said, though his all-round quality had never been in doubt, arguably he never surpassed his first two Ashton Gate campaigns.

Mickey Bell began his professional career as a trainee with Northampton Town before switching to Wycombe in 1994. His arrival at City three years later, in a £150,000 deal settled by a transfer tribunal, was something of a surprise after he had won the Wanderers' player of the season award. The Robins' boss, John Ward, was practically salivating at the prospect of harnessing Mickey with Darren Barnard on the left flank, with yet another 'leftie', Brian Tinnion, adopting a slightly more central role.

During pre-season the combination gelled as mighty Liverpool were run ragged, but the trio never played a competitive game together as Darren accepted his Premiership move to Barnsley. Nevertheless City remained fabulously effective down the left, with Mickey taking over free-kick duties and helping to fire City to promotion in his first season at the club.

He featured in the PFA Division Two team of that campaign and was one of the most regular recipients of such divisional accolades in recent terms, too. Tellingly, in the solitary and rocky year in Division One, Mickey shone as one of City's few consistent performers. His form dipped slightly after the drop to Division Two, but after being jolted by being placed on the transfer list, he responded by returning to his peak.

Still, when his contract ended in 2004, Bell thought his time might be up. However, before he had even considered his options, Brian Tinnion – his team-mate, friend and greatest advocate – was appointed as Danny Wilson's replacement. Duly Brian helped convince his fellow north-easterner to carry on another year, during which the full-back took his total of League and cup appearances for the club past the 300 mark. Another extension was not proffered, and he departed for Port Vale, but it would have taken a brave man to tell Mickey Bell to call it a day.

JUNIOR BENT

1989/90 — 1997/98

JUNIOR BENT was a bookie's living nightmare, and Bristol City loved him for it. When the diminutive winger pulled on the red shirt, form books were booted further out of Ashton Gate than some of his gob-smacking misses in front of goal. The only certainty about Junior was that whatever he did would be done in a hurry. Regular supporters lost count of the occasions when his searing pace would leave defenders chasing dust, but as the goal beckoned for the seemingly inevitable strike, somehow he would manage to punt the ball into the far reaches of the Atyeo Stand.

Chances were plentiful for Junior, however, and frequently he would convert the most difficult one after missing the simplest. It was this glorious unpredictability paired with his unrelenting enthusiasm that made him one of the most enduring fans' favourites in recent memory.

No one was ever more thrilled to be playing for City than Junior Bent, and it showed. He was immensely popular with coaches, players and journalists, as well as the fans; his work ethic on the training pitch was phenomenal and on matchdays he would strive even harder. Not surprisingly for a fellow measuring little more than 5ft in his football socks, heading was not his strong suit, but he ensured that every other element of his game was practised diligently.

Ironically it was the effervescent Yorkshireman's fervent longing to do well that often proved his undoing, and sometimes he tried too hard, so that nothing would go his way. When he was relaxed he was devastating, but when he was nervous he could be a liability.

As a quick, right-sided midfielder, Junior spent his formative years as a trainee at Huddersfield under the tutelage of former Ashton Gate favourite Gordon Low. He made a handful of senior appearances for the Terriers before a loan spell at Burnley, where he caught the eye of Robins boss Joe Jordan, who signed him on transfer deadline day in 1990.

The eager newcomer watched from the sidelines as City secured promotion to the old Second Division, then featured frequently at senior level during the following year. However, it was not until 1993/94 that Junior truly came of age in a football sense, attaining cult status in the stands and playing an integral part in the club's progress to the last 16 of the FA Cup. During the unforgettable 1-0 win against Liverpool he was hailed as City's star man, despite Brian Tinnion's stunning goal. That night he gave the Merseysiders' rearguard a comprehensive chasing, especially Scottish international Steve Nicol, who had been handed the unenviable task of marking him.

It came as a surprise when Junior moved on in 1997, announcing his intention of seeking fresh pastures at Blackpool only 24 hours after being offered a new City deal. Thus the team had lost one of its most willing members, but at least he had contrived a fitting send-off, rising from the bench in his final match to supply the goal which knocked Bristol Rovers out of the League Cup.

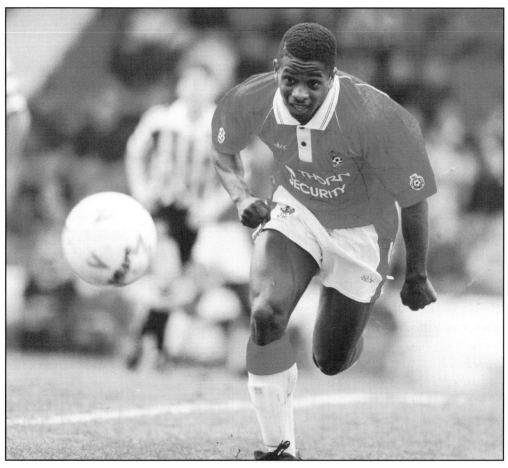

BORN: Huddersfield, Yorkshire, 1.3.70

CITY RECORD:

League: 142 (41) games, 20 goals

FA Cup: 12 (3) games, 2 goals

League Cup: 10 (3) games, 1 goal

Others: 7 (3) games, 0 goals

Total: 171 (50) games, 23 goals

OTHER CLUBS:

Huddersfield Town 87/8-89/90 (36, 6)

Burnley on loan 89/90 (9, 3)

Stoke City on loan 91/2 (1, 0)

Shrewsbury Town on loan 96/7 (6, 0)

Blackpool 97/8-99/00 (103, 5)

BORN: Cradley, Birmingham, 31.5.31

CITY RECORD:

League: 205 games, 34 goals

FA Cup: 7 games, 0 goals

League Cup: 1 game, 1 goal

Total: 213 games, 35 goals

CITY HONOURS:

Third Division South Championship 54/5

OTHER CLUBS:

Coventry City 56/7-59/60 (90, 17)

JACK BOXLEY

1950/51 — 1956/57 & 1960/61

JACK BOXLEY'S LEFT FOOT was the subject of much debate in the early and middle 1950s. Some soccer pundits reckoned he could paint with it, others that it could open a tin of beans, while still more referred to it as educated. However, one thing on which they all agreed was that it was one of the most lethal attacking weapons in the Bristol City armoury.

Its owner was a stylish, speedy winger whose gloriously accurate crosses and rasping shots were invaluable to the Robins for several seasons, his most devastating form coinciding happily with the 1954/55 Third Division South Championship campaign.

Pat Beasley signed Jack from Stourbridge in August 1950 in the face of strong competition from rival clubs. After handing over a cheque for £2,000, a stiff fee for a non-League player, the City manager predicted that the skilful winger would make a swift impact on fans and full-backs alike; and he was right. Although he was not one to relish the most ferocious of challenges, and team-mates joked that he wouldn't head the ball for fear of damaging his perfect set of teeth, Jack had the ability to be a match-winner.

His supply of centres to the likes of Arnold Rodgers and John Atyeo – he gave John additional service as best man at his wedding –

resulted in many goals, and the side was noticeably weaker during his frequent absences through knee problems during his early years at Ashton Gate. Jack's appearance record improved after operations on both knees and he missed only a handful of matches for three seasons, including the club's first in the Second Division.

An expert in dead-ball situations, Jack was the Robins' penalty-taker for 18 months, bagging six in 1953/54 alone; but perhaps his most memorable goal came in the dying minutes of the home encounter with Watford in November 1954. The game was goalless at that point – thanks largely to City full-back Ivor Guy, deputising between the posts for the injured Tony Cook – when Jack made his decisive strike, thundering home a Jimmy Rogers pass from 20 yards to send the crowd into ecstasies.

In December 1956 the Boxley-Rogers tandem moved to Coventry, Jimmy returning two years later, Jack in 1960. By then, however, Boxley's prime was past, and he was unable to compete with young Jantzen Derrick for a first-team slot. Instead, the friendly Midlander retired and went on to become a car salesman just around the corner from Ashton Gate.

ALEC BRIGGS

1957/58 — 1969/70

WHEN ALEC BRIGGS made up his mind to do something, then invariably he did it. Whether it was securing a place in the Bristol City side and holding it for a decade, coming out on top in a 50-50 challenge or, in later years, building up a successful business, the Yorkshire-born full-back was a study in determination.

Alec, whose habitually grim expression on the field concealed an affable nature, needed every grain of resolution as a teenager at Ashton Gate. After being drafted into the side at Cardiff in April 1958 – lining up behind a fellow debutant, right-half Peter McCall – he suffered a swift return to the reserves. Manager Peter Doherty signed right-backs Gordon Hopkinson and Roger Collinson in quick succession, and suddenly a future that had seemed so bright took on a distinctly darker hue.

While the senior side lurched towards relegation to the Third Division, Alec, a dedicated athlete whose fitness was a byword throughout his career, fought to win back his place. Frustrated by his situation, he eventually became a part-timer, his lively mind perhaps needing more stimulation than second-string football could provide. But he never lost sight of his soccer ambition, and was coached by club skipper Tommy Burden, who always retained faith in his ability.

Ironically, only a few months after Alec took a job outside the game, new City boss Fred Ford was impressed by the right-footer's willingness to have a go on the left flank, and called him up as a deputy for Mike Thresher. He played well and was in the team to stay, initially in the number-two slot but later reverting to left-back when Mike retired and Tony Ford broke through.

Alec, who played a stalwart part in the Robins' rise to Division Two in 1964/65, was a consistent performer not given to the limelight, although one display against Aston Villa's highly-rated Harry Burrows in an FA Cup clash at an icy Ashton Gate in January 1963 did take the eye. That night, as ever, Alec was stern in the tackle, but his shackling of such an elusive opponent on a treacherous surface attracted extra praise.

His faults were few; he might occasionally have been slow to recover when passed by a nippy winger, and in the early days the quality of his passing was indifferent. Overall, however, Alec was an admirable servant to the City cause, and a credit to his profession. Football would be infinitely the richer for more men like him.

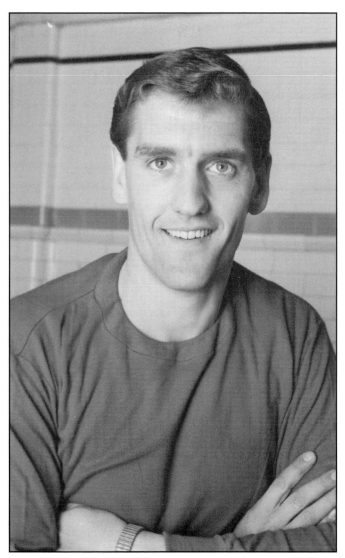

BORN: Sheffield, 21.6.39

CITY RECORD:

League: 349 (2) games, 1 goal

FA Cup: 29 games, 0 goals

League Cup: 14 games, 0 goals

Others: 1 game, 1 goal

Total: 393 (2) games, 2 goals

CITY HONOURS:

Promoted from Third Division 64/5

BORN: Andover, Hampshire, 21.2.24

DIED: Street, Somerset, 10.01

CITY RECORD:

League: 231 games, 20 goals

FA Cup: 12 games, 1 goal

Total: 243 games, 21 goals

CITY HONOURS:

Third Division South Championship 54/5

OTHER CLUBS:

Chester 45/6-47/8 (82, 39)

Leeds United 48/9-54/5 (243, 13)

TOMMY BURDEN

1954/55 – 1960/61

BRISTOL CITY MANAGER Pat Beasley must have blessed the autumn day in 1954 that Tommy Burden, a born leader and superbly efficient wing-half cum inside-forward, decided he could no longer live in Somerset and play for Leeds United.

Thirty-year-old Tommy, who had been brought up in the West Country and planned to live there when his football career was over, had taken a job in Street while continuing at Elland Road. When the constant travelling became impracticable, he left the Yorkshire club but was willing to return to League football on a part-time basis. To Pat, whose side was topping the Third Division South table by October but was still in urgent need of class and experience, this was a windfall indeed.

Accordingly, the Robins signed the former Leeds skipper for £1,500 down, plus £500 for each of the next three years if he remained in the team. In fact Tommy stayed at Ashton Gate for seven seasons, including several as captain, and his impact was immeasurable as he helped City win promotion as Champions in his first term, and then survive in the Second Division until the end of the decade.

As an all-round footballer he barely had a weakness, bringing craft, graft and persistence to the team's engine room. A quick thinker and improviser, he could control and pass the ball accurately with either foot, there was steel in his tackling, and despite the advancing years he was not devoid of pace.

Tommy was noted more for consistency than dazzling individual contributions, although there were some notable exceptions. One was his driving, all-action display, including a goal, in a 6-4 victory over Blackburn at Ewood Park in October 1955, though perhaps even more memorable was his dribble past a posse of Bristol Rovers defenders to equalise in an FA Cup thriller eventually won by the Pirates at Ashton Gate in February 1958.

A strong-willed though pleasant character, Tommy – who played in wartime competitions for Wolves before joining the Army and being wounded in the D-Day landings – was a dedicated professional and a natural football teacher who would have been perfect managerial material had he not already mapped out his future in the shoe trade.

By the time he retired from the game to devote himself to full-time business, he had established himself as one of the most influential figures in the Robins' post-war history.

BORN: Bristol, 20.1.77

CITY RECORD:

League: 315 (11) games, 5 goals

FA Cup: 18 (1) games, 0 goals

League Cup: 15 (1) games, 0 goals

Others: 21 (2) games, 1 goal

Total: 369 (15) games, 6 goals

CITY HONOURS:

Promotion from Second Division 97/8

LDV Vans Trophy 02/03

Auto Windscreens Shield Finalist 99/00

OTHER CLUBS:

Coventry City 04/05 (23, 0)

LOUIS CAREY

1995/96 — 2003/04 & 2004/05 —

LOUIS CAREY was a man determined to prove that nice guys do not finish last. Brought up a City supporter, the versatile defender had been a mainstay in the side since breaking into the first-team under Joe Jordan in 1995. The club could not have wished for a more loyal, honest and popular servant. But like many love-affairs, this one hit a rocky patch.

Tempers were frayed at Ashton Gate after the play-off final defeat against Brighton in 2004. Louis's contract had run out and he could not come to an agreement on a new one, even though the club and the player both stated their wish to stay together. As City's most senior home-grown talent, Carey felt justified in holding out for wage parity with some of the Robins' new, but less loyal signings. As a result the usually amiable Bristolian was ordered to train at home in exile, which he did until Peter Reid's Coventry City came calling.

The outcry from City fans after Louis left was testament to a popular character who had time for everyone at the club. He was always the last man on to the coach returning from away games because he spent so long talking over the side's progress with travelling supporters.

His team-mates held him in equally fond regard – even though they were often the butt of his endless practical jokes. Along with close friend Scott Murray, he juggled his role as irrepressible japester with a responsible awareness that he was a role model to the impressionable young academy players.

It was little surprise when, only six months after their acrimonious parting, Louis Carey and Bristol City kissed and made up. Both sides admitted they had said things they didn't really mean, and the 28-year-old took a pay cut to come home.

Louis started his career at right-back but it was in the centre of defence, where his understanding with Shaun Taylor verged on the uncanny, that he began to earn plaudits. Carey's compelling combination of pace, spring and anticipation made up for a lack of height and his tackling was invariably clean and accurate. He was susceptible to the odd heart-stopping moments due to over-ambitious dribbling but his excellent progress during the 1998 promotion campaign earned him a call up for the Scottish under-21 squad.

After Danny Wilson arrived at Ashton Gate, Louis barely missed a game, making the right-back berth his own. With young Danny Coles, Matt Hill and Steve Phillips breaking through, City's homegrown rearguard became one of the best in the country. In 2003/04 no club outside the top flight boasted a tighter defence and Carey's organisational skills were a major part of that. His efforts were recognised when he was named in the Division Two team of the year, but the acknowledgement he had yearned for – in the shape of a lucrative new contract – was never to arrive.

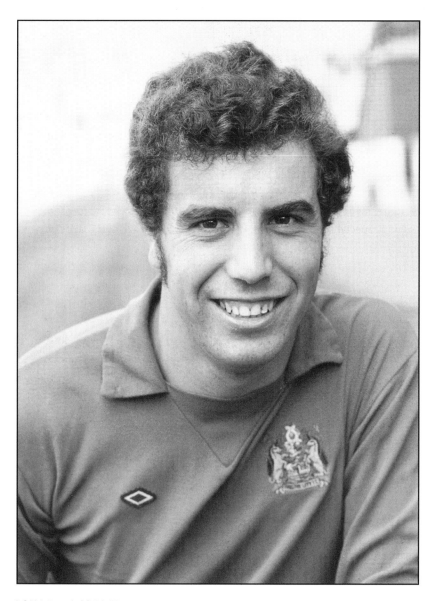

BORN: Bristol, 23.10.51

CITY RECORD:

League: 227 games, 1 goal

FA Cup: 9 games, 0 goals

League Cup: 11 games, 0 goal

Others: 14 (1) games, 0 goals

Total: 261 (1) games, 1 goal

CITY HONOURS:

Promotion from Second Division 75/6

OTHER CLUBS:

Hereford United on loan 80/1 (20, 0)

Bristol Rovers 83/4-84/5 (53, 0)

Chester City (non-contract) 85/6 (9, 0)

RAY CASHLEY

1970/71 — 1980/81

RAY CASHLEY became a goalkeeper by accident. The man who was to star between the Robins' posts as they won promotion to the First Division in 1975/76 was attracting scant attention as a distinctly mundane teenage left-back when Bristol City Youths were faced with a sudden crisis.

Regular custodian Len Bond suffered a kidney injury during a cup run and there was no time to sign a specialist replacement. An impromptu trial was staged and Ray revealed hitherto unsuspected acrobatic talents to earn the green jersey. So well did he do that within months he had turned professional in his new role, and, with Mike Gibson nearing the end of his City tenure, it wasn't long before the former number-three was challenging for senior recognition.

After making his debut in a 3-0 FA Cup defeat at Southampton in January 1970, Ray made steady progress, responding well to intensive coaching sessions with manager Alan Dicks and continuing to learn his trade as a first-teamer. In the early days he cut an awkward figure and was nicknamed 'The Bear' for his rough-and-ready way of shifting teammates and opponents alike from his path. But respect was not long in coming as Ray showed exceptional bravery in diving among the boots, sharp reflexes on his line and confidence in punching the ball.

It was another Cashley speciality, his long kick, that brought an unexpected bonus one windy Ashton Gate night in 1973, when Ray's towering clearance deceived his Hull counterpart Jeff Wealands and bounced into the net for his first and only goal.

The muscular Bristolian's major weakness was in judging when to forsake his six-yard area to claim crosses, and there were times when he was caught in no-man's land. Such rash forays could be costly, as Manchester City's Denis Tueart demonstrated with a subtle chip to take the points at Maine Road in September 1976.

Against this must be placed many match-winning performances, especially in the two terms before reaching the top flight, when Ray kept clean sheets in the face of heavy bombardment. One of his most impressive showings was in a goalless draw at Upton Park, in which he saved a penalty and a series of scorching drives.

In the higher grade his form was patchy and he fell behind John Shaw and Jan Moller, leaving City for a year out of the game before putting in spells with Bristol Rovers and Chester. Ray Cashley's career stands as a monument to the glorious uncertainty of football.

BORN: Easton-in-Gordano, Bristol, 20.10.53

CITY RECORD:

League: 61 (3) games, 20 goals

FA Cup: 2 games, 0 goals

League Cup: 4 games, 1 goal

Others: 6 games, 0 goals

Total: 73 (3) games, 21 goals

CITY HONOURS:

Promotion from Second Division 75/6

OTHER CLUBS:

Norwich City 72/3-73/4 (13, 1)

PAUL CHEESLEY

1973/74 — 1976/77

THERE IS NO SHORTAGE of shrewd observers who maintain that Bristol City were doomed to struggle for First Division survival from the moment Paul Cheesley's burgeoning career was cut short by injury. Their argument is a persuasive one. On arrival among the elite, the Robins were tight at the back, with a competitive and tolerably creative midfield; all they needed was goal power, a quality the dynamic young centre-forward was admirably equipped to provide.

The omens were auspicious as Paul made a sensational impact in City's top-flight opener against Arsenal in August 1976. He subjected classy Irish international centre-back David O'Leary to an afternoon of torment in the Highbury sunshine, establishing utter supremacy in the air and scoring the only goal of the game with a thumping header.

Only a few months earlier England manager Don Revie, on the evidence of Paul's form in the Second Division promotion campaign, had dubbed him the most improved player in the country and elevated him to the under-23 squad. A League game had deprived him of his first international chance, but there seemed little doubt that a breakthrough was imminent.

Paul's splendid showings in 1975/76 had surprised many who had written him off as a carthorse after he had floundered for 18 months on making a £30,000 move to his native West Country from Norwich in December 1973. Yet Alan Dicks had retained faith that the burly striker had all the necessary qualifications for the big time, and the City boss was proved to be an impeccable judge.

Paul possessed a fierce shot in either foot, was working hard on his ball skills, and was explosively quick in the short bursts so vital to penalty-area predators. But it was in aerial combat that he was revealed in his full majesty. Paul's great gift was a sense of timing – sometimes it created the optical illusion that he was hanging in the air – which afforded him an extra split-second in which to direct the ball goalwards or nod it to partner Tom Ritchie.

The future beckoned alluringly, but three days after the glory of Highbury came disaster at Ashton Gate. Paul twisted his knee in a collision with Stoke City's Peter Shilton, and, apart from one ill-fated attempt at a comeback two months later, he was lost to League football forever.

Bristol City never found a comparable replacement and, so the theory goes, the decline was under way. Four years later the Robins were relegated. The primary cause? Lack of punch at the front . . .

BORN: Bristol, 13.1.43

CITY RECORD:

League: 195 games, 83 goals

FA Cup: 14 games, 6 goals

League Cup: 6 games, 0 goals

Total: 215 games, 89 goals

CITY HONOURS:

Promotion from Third Division 64/5

OTHER CLUBS:

Huddersfield Town 66/7-67/8 (32, 11)

Cardiff City 67/8-72/3 (182, 75)

Bournemouth 72/3-73/4 (30, 12)

Millwall 73/4-74/5 (71, 16)

Cardiff City 75/6 (21, 1)

Newport County 76/7-78/9 (80, 18)

BRIAN CLARK

WHEN JOHN ATYEO RETIRED after 15 years as Ashton Gate's marksman-in-chief, there seemed little doubt about the identity of his long-term successor. For four seasons Brian Clark had been learning at the master's elbow and matching him goal for goal, his all-round aptitude for the game attracting interest from some of the country's leading clubs and taking him to the fringe of the England under-23 squad.

Yet after suffering a lean spell in the early months of 1966/67 – the first campaign after John's departure – the 23-year-old Bristolian was allowed to join Huddersfield Town in exchange for ageing midfielder John Quigley and £2,500. The little Scot gave the Robins, floundering at the wrong end of the Second Division, a much-needed boost; but there was dismay among many supporters at manager Fred Ford's decision to dispense with the services of the blond striker.

Brian – whose father, Don, had been a prolific City centre-forward in the immediate post-war years – took over the role of Atyeo's apprentice in the early 1960s, with Bobby Williams completing an inside-trio of rare enterprise.

Clark Jnr, sturdily built and standing an inch under six feet, lacked exceptional pace but little else. He was brave, packed a fierce shot in either foot, was strong in the air and was supremely unselfish, doing much of the legwork for Big John, by then in his thirties. Brian's close control and neat distribution were ideally suited to the slick one-two passing movements relished by the England international, and together they were a formidable proposition for most defences.

The partnership was particularly effective during the Robins' climb out of the Third Division in 1964/65, with both men scoring in the promotion-clinching game against Oldham at Ashton Gate, and again on arrival in the higher flight. When Brian suffered the goal drought that led to his sale, there were those who reckoned he couldn't play without the retired Atyeo. His subsequent record with five other clubs – notably at Cardiff, in harness with John Toshack – made nonsense of such simplistic thinking.

Brian, whose honest approach and amiable personality made him liked and respected throughout the game, had merely suffered the temporary loss of form and confidence that afflicts all strikers from time to time. The fact that he was still scoring goals in the Football League some 12 years after his Ashton Gate exit would seem to prove the point.

DON CLARK

1938/39 — 1950/51

BRISTOL CITY have been blessed with a plethora of prolific goal-scorers since the war. John Atyeo and Arnold Rodgers, John Galley and Bob Taylor, Andy Cole and Leroy Lita, they have all enjoyed periods of plenty, and Ashton Gate fans have revelled in their exploits.

But none of them could ever match the feat of Don Clark in 1946/47. During that exhilarating campaign in which the Robins narrowly missed promotion to the Second Division, the dashing blond centre-forward scored 36 times in 37 games, a club record, and chipped in with five strikes in two FA Cup outings for good measure.

Don's magnificent achievement in topping the 40-goal mark overall, even more remarkable in view of a five-match spell in which he was sidelined by injury, did provoke one supremely frustrating reflection. During that term he celebrated his 29th birthday, having lost the previous seven seasons to the war, and there was little left of his prime in which to make the most of such a precious talent.

Clark Snr had made his League debut for City in 1939. At that time he was a relatively recent convert from the game of rugby, having taken up soccer only after leaving school, and usually played at wing-half. In the course of wartime competition Robins boss Bob Hewison recognised his true potential, and a marksman was born.

Don was well endowed with the tools of his new trade, possessing pace, strength, a fair amount of skill and exceptional balance. He could hit the ball sweetly with either foot, though his right was the more lethal, and had a priceless knack of keeping his shots low, an ability feared by most goalkeepers.

As if his goals were not enough to endear him to the fans, Don also charmed them with his personality. He was an amiable soul who enjoyed taking the mickey, and was also a scrupulously honourable footballer, the type who would make Roy of the Rovers look like a cheat.

His playing days were effectively ended when he damaged his knee in a collision with a Leyton Orient defender at Brisbane Road in February 1949. There were brief comebacks in each of the next two seasons, but the old zip had departed and he retired to become the club's assistant secretary until 1956.

Then Don, whose son Brian became a star City striker in the 1960s, took a job outside the game and was left to ponder on what glory might have been his if the heart had not been torn from a career that was in its infancy when the lights went out.

BORN: Bristol, 25.10.17

CITY RECORD:

League: 117 games, 67 goals

FA Cup: 19 games, 15 goals

Total: 136 games, 82 goals

ANDY COLE

ISN'T IT AMAZING what some people throw out? Many believed Andy Cole's career was in decline before it had really started when the raw, unpredictable striker was abruptly discarded by mighty Arsenal. Yet by the time he left Bristol City to return to the bright lights of the new Premier League he was one of the hottest young properties in the game. City were always likely to be a temporary stepping stone for a player of his refined talents, but still their fans can boast that one of the great British goal-scorers of the modern era chose Ashton Gate as the arena to introduce himself to the footballing world.

Undoubtedly it was to the Robins' advantage that Cole arrived in south Bristol with a size-able point to prove, particularly to Arsenal boss George Graham. After progressing through the ranks at the north London club he had been tipped for a prosperous future at Highbury, his ability to move the ball from his feet and get a shot away within the blink of an eye being a sign of a striker of the highest calibre. But fellow rookie Kevin Campbell looked like he might become a world-beater and Ian Wright was clearly top-class so, in effect, Graham faced a stark choice between Cole and Campbell. The dour Scot chose Campbell, who had fitted in better at the club and offered a greater aerial presence alongside the more compact Wright.

Andy was still just 20 at that point and it was the type of rejection which could have broken a lesser man. However, the Midlander was blessed with an abundance of self-belief, and it was to prove justified.

After his arrival at Ashton Gate in the spring of 1992 – initially on loan, but eventually in exchange for a £500,000 cheque – Cole supplied the goals to steer City away from relegation, and in his second season at the club he was a joy to watch alongside the equally idolised maverick Jackie Dziekanowski.

Seldom in City's history had fans been treated to a more dynamic and exciting front pairing than Andy and Jackie. Their intuitive understanding was spellbinding, with Cole's pace and direct running offering the perfect contrast to Dziekanowski's more subtle build-up play. All too rapidly successive City managers Denis Smith and Russell Osman were inundated with approaches for the precocious youngster, and Division One pace-setters Newcastle emerged as the successful suitors.

His £1.75 million move in March 1993 proved a spectacular success, and soon the rising star was worshipped on Tyneside. His confidence appeared to grow with each goal as promotion was secured, then he took the top flight by storm. His brilliant link with Peter Beardsley threw up comparisons with 'the Jackie partnership' and City fans were not surprised as Andy became one of Europe's top scorers in 1993/94.

After a lucrative transfer to Manchester United he went on to fill his trophy cabinet with almost every bauble available, and was still holding his own in the Premiership with Fulham in 2005. Point proved, Mr Graham?

BORN: Nottingham, 15.10.71

CITY RECORD:

League: 41 games, 20 goals

FA Cup: 1 game, 0 goals

League Cup: 3 games, 4 goals

Others: 4 games, 1 goal

Total: 49 games, 25 goals

OTHER CLUBS:

Arsenal 90/1 (1, 0)

Fulham on loan 91/2 (13, 3)

Newcastle United 92/3-94/5 (70, 55)

Manchester United 94/5-01/02 (195, 93)

Blackburn Rovers 01/02-03/04 (83, 27)

Fulham 04/05 (31, 12)

Manchester City 05/06-

15 England caps 1995-2001

GARY COLLIER

1972/73 — 1978/79

GARY COLLIER was an enterprising young man, both on and off the field. As a cultured centre-half of the Alan Hansen school he dropped hints of international potential; as an individual seeking his football fortune he was never loth to take unorthodox decisions, a trait that was to lead him out of the British game and deprive him of all but the most slender chance of entering the England reckoning.

The elegant Bristolian made his debut as an 18-year-old in March 1973, deputising for the injured Geoff Merrick, and it was instantly clear that a performer of such skill, pace and intelligence must soon claim a regular place. Sure enough he did, slotting alongside Geoff at the expense of David Rodgers, and a glittering future appeared to beckon.

Loose and limber of movement, Gary was a superb athlete who seemed to flow over the ground with a grace denied to most defenders, though his mobility was not always a guarantee of success. When standing in at full-back against Bolton at Burnden Park in January 1974 he was given a torrid first half by wily veteran Peter Thompson. He was, however, a quick learner, and countered the former England star far more effectively after the interval.

The one flaw in Gary's game was that for a six-footer he was not particularly dominant with his head. When partnered by the spring-heeled Merrick this was of little consequence, but when Norman Hunter – himself no aerial kingpin – arrived shortly after promotion to the First Division there were times when the Robins' rearguard looked vulnerable. As a result, in the spring of 1978 David Rodgers was recalled to replace Gary, who spent most of the following campaign in the reserves.

It was at the end of that season that the Collier initiative asserted itself. Gary became the first English player to change clubs under the new freedom-of-contract regulations, negotiating his own deal with Coventry City, who paid the Robins £325,000. However, his tenure at Highfield Road was destined to be short; after two games and a difference of opinion with Sky Blues boss Gordon Milne, Gary was pondering the chances of a return to Ashton Gate when in stepped American club Portland Timbers with an offer he couldn't refuse.

Coventry banked £365,000, then the biggest fee for any English player to cross the Atlantic, and Gary was Stateside bound. Thus did a 24-year-old with the talent, temperament and stature of a top-class centre-half opt out of the soccer mainstream.

BORN: Bristol, 4.2.55

CITY RECORD:

League: 193 games, 3 goals

FA Cup: 11 games, 0 goals

League Cup: 11 games, 0 goals

Others: 15 (1) games, 0 goals

Total: 230 (1) games, 3 goals

CITY HONOURS:

Promotion from Second Division 75/6

Anglo-Scottish Cup 77/8

OTHER CLUBS:

Coventry City 79/80 (2, 0)

Portland Timbers, USA

San Diego, USA

JACK CONNOR

1960/61 — 1970/71

THE 1960S would have been an infinitely duller decade at Ashton Gate without Big Jack Connor. Radiating resolution and good cheer, he stood four-square at the heart of the Bristol City defence for more than 400 games, a swashbuckling, larger-than-life figure whose very presence lifted the spirits of team-mates and supporters alike.

Somehow Jack put football in the right perspective. During a game or a training session, he was the ultimate professional and no one would strive harder in the Robins' interests. But afterwards it was time for a joke and a chat, and it was rare to catch him without a huge smile on his face.

The tall, muscular Cumbrian headed southwest from Huddersfield Town in one of the shrewdest transfer deals ever completed by City boss Fred Ford. The man who was to be the side's defensive bulwark for ten seasons was secured in a straight swap for Johnny McCann, a Scottish winger who had failed to settle in Bristol after moving down from Barnsley.

Jack, who relished surging forward for set pieces, took over from Alan Williams at centre-half and soon introduced a new solidity to an alarmingly shaky rearguard. He was dominant in the air – the wide Connor forehead might have been custom-built for smacking a football from penalty area to half-way line – and powerful in the tackle, with a fair turn of pace despite an ungainly, splayed gait. Jack was never a man to dwell on the ball and his clearances were instant, either a long-distance whack or a short pass to a more constructive colleague.

As the 1960s progressed, his understanding with City's relatively small 'keeper Mike Gibson grew ever more impressive, Jack dealing with most of the crosses and Mike patrolling his immediate goal area. The partnership seemed almost telepathic at times – despite the odd occasion when a wild slice from the centre-half's boot would sneak past his stranded colleague – and it was a crucial factor in the Robins' Third Division promotion triumph in 1964/65.

Come the 1970s, and 35-year-old Jack stepped aside in favour of Dickie Rooks before taking up coaching, first with City and then, briefly, with Everton. Later he took a job outside the game and lived in the north-west, though whenever he returned to Bristol his welcome was warm. At Ashton Gate his stock remains as high as ever; Jack would never utter a word against anyone, and to this day there isn't a soul who would say a word against him.

BORN: Maryport, Cumberland, 25.7.34

CITY RECORD:

League: 354 (1) games, 10 goals

FA Cup: 35 games, 2 goals

League Cup: 14 games, 0 goals

Others: 2 games, 0 goals

Total: 405 (1) games, 12 goals

CITY HONOURS:

Promotion from Third Division 64/5

OTHER CLUBS:

Huddersfield Town 54/5-60/1 (85, 10)

BORN: Bristol, 8.10.29

DIED: Bristol, 3.96

CITY RECORD:

League: 320 games, 0 goals

FA Cup: 22 games, 0 goals

League Cup: 4 games, 0 goals

Others: 2 games, 0 goals

Total: 348 games, 0 goals

CITY HONOURS:

Third Division South Championship 54/5

TONY COOK

1952/53 — 1963/64

TONY COOK was the Robins goalkeeper who doubled as club comedian, but there was never the slightest chance of the two roles overlapping. When he was between the posts the ebullient Bristolian was a serious and fiercely committed custodian, one of the finest City have had. Off duty, Tony was one of the funniest men in football, a cheerful mixer with the fans and just the sort of chap to divert his team-mates on those tedious marathon coach journeys of pre-motorway days.

He made his debut in November 1952, and it was quickly obvious that this wisecracking recruit from the local Downs League was an outstanding prospect. Tony was strong and brave enough to look after himself in an era when 'keepers were not mollycoddled by referees, and he was an acrobatic shot-stopper.

But it was his confidence in claiming crosses that really took the eye. Occasionally he was prone to rushes of blood, as in a clash with Shrewsbury when he caught a centre outside his penalty area, but brilliant performances were far more common, and one, against Newport at Ashton Gate in December 1953, had the press proclaiming that he had taken on the Welshmen on his own.

Despite his extrovert personality, Tony was tense before games, often indulging in a Woodbine to calm his nerves; usually he would nip into the toilets to avoid being caught by manager Fred Ford, a fervent anti-smoker. Good-naturedly he endured a lot of ribbing about this pre-match habit and could take a joke as well as the next man, but he was once hurt by a mischievous and utterly preposterous story that he had been drunk during a match. The lie was propagated that he had been boozing on the team coach before and after the 5-0 defeat at Plymouth on Boxing Day 1955. In fact, City had travelled to the match by train and Tony hadn't touched a drop of alcohol, but for years the unjustified slur on his professional conduct was thrown in his face.

That incident probably upset him even more than the broken arm that removed him from the run-in to the Third Division South Championship in 1954/55 and prompted Bob Anderson's arrival as a replacement. But Tony fought back to regain his first-team spot and play nearly 350 senior games for the Robins before moving into non-League football and ultimately returning to the Downs League. In 1989 he retired after 23 years as a prison officer in Bristol, his sense of humour as sharp as ever. In any walk of life Tony Cook, who died in 1996, would have been an entertainer.

BORN: Bristol, 10.1.43

CITY RECORD:

League: 254 (6) games, 32 goals

FA Cup: 25 games, 4 goals

League Cup: 11 (1) games, 0 goals

Others: 2 games, 0 goals

Total: 292 (7) games, 36 goals

OTHER CLUBS:

Mansfield Town on loan 70/1 (2, 0)

Paris St Germain

JANTZEN DERRICK

1959/60 — 1970/71

IF SUBLIME NATURAL GIFTS were enough to make a great player, then Jantzen Derrick would have won England caps by the dozen and graced the higher echelons of the Football League. But they aren't, and he didn't, and to successive Bristol City managers, team-mates and fans fell the frustrating lot of watching a prodigious talent drift towards oblivion. Jantzen was the classic example of a soccer sorcerer who would flit past three defenders only to lose possession to the fourth, or attempt to thread a nigh-impossible pass through a crowd of opponents when a simple push to a better placed colleague would have been more effective.

Yet it all began so promisingly. After starring for England Schoolboys, Jantzen broke into the Ashton Gate senior side at 16; his appearance on the left wing at Lincoln in November 1959 made him City's youngest ever debutant. Within a year he was regularly part of the newly-relegated Robins' Third Division line-up and manager Fred Ford eagerly took on the task of harnessing the teenager's extravagant ability, with mixed results. For two matches Jantzen might illuminate proceedings in breathtaking style, whetting the appetites of several leading clubs. Then he would slump into anonymity for the next three.

Fred kept faith with him, often in the face of severe criticism from supporters who questioned his work rate, bravery and motivation, though there were occasions when the boss's patience ran out. In February 1964 Jantzen was told to turn on the magic or be dropped; with beguiling inevitability, he gave one of his finest displays to inspire a home thrashing of Wrexham. But he could not achieve consistency on either left or right flank, and was sidelined for most of the 1964/65 promotion campaign by Ray Savino and Roger Peters. In the Second Division he regained his place but continued to tantalise, and his City career finally withered under the pragmatic regime of Alan Dicks.

There followed a short interlude with Paris St Germain before Jantzen returned to Bristol and took a job outside the game. His failure to reach the heights saddened all who revel in pure skill. It may have been that his ball control was so complete and his vision so sharp that this relaxed, almost whimsical soccer artist simply could not resist attempting the most difficult and ambitious of manoeuvres. Unfortunately the trait of tilting at windmills, though endearingly attractive, is out of tune with the harsh reality of professional football.

BORN: Bristol, 17.3.79

CITY RECORD:

League: 156 (33) games, 7 goals

FA Cup: 7 (1) games, 0 goals

League Cup: 9 (1) games, 1 goal

Others: 18 (1) games, 1 goal

Total: 190 (36) games, 9 goals

CITY HONOURS:

Promotion from Second Division 97/8

LDV Vans Trophy 02/03

OTHER CLUBS:

Queen's Park Rangers 05/06-

8 Northern Ireland caps 2003-

TOMMY DOHERTY

1997/98 — 2004/05

TOMMY DOHERTY offered a refreshing change from the preening prima-donna attitude which characterises so many modern footballers. The Bedminster-born lad never craved the fame, glamour and adulation associated with a top sportsman; he just loved to play, usually with his heart displayed prominently on his sleeve. Like many of City's enigmatic heroes down the decades, however, Tommy was gloriously unpredictable. While his all-round abilities might have dictated a fast-track to the highest echelons of the game, something always held him back.

With his scruffy hair and unshaven face, the proud Bristolian's abrasive playing style was often as much wild man of the woods as midfield maestro. Yet that fierce persona on the pitch was in stark contrast with his modest and shy character off it. Tommy was always a private man who invariably did his best to steer clear of interviews. Some believed he was just not interested in grabbing headlines, while others put his singular approach down to a dreadful time with injuries which left him paranoid about tempting fate in print or on the air.

It's reasonable to speculate that if it wasn't for his seemingly constant fitness problems, City's indomitable midfield general would have been pursued incessantly by Premiership clubs. With each passing season, his importance to the Robins grew in the same way as his hero Roy Keane's had for Manchester United. Like Keane, Doherty was often at his most majestic when the odds were stacked against him, and despite his diminutive frame, there were few players in League One who could have been backed to beat him in a 50-50

challenge during 2004/05. Deservedly he became a regular in the Northern Ireland side and distinguished himself in their stirring 0-0 draw with Spain.

Tommy was one of a handful of youngsters to break into the first team during Joe Jordan's second reign at Ashton Gate, and one particularly eye-catching display against Leeds in the League Cup earned him an instant seal of approval from supporters. That autumn evening at Ashton Gate Doherty brimmed with brio and defiance, meeting Premiership class with his own persuasive cocktail of crunching tackles and pinpoint passes.

Tommy's popularity soared even further later in that 1997/98 campaign when the combative play-maker earned an extended spell in the side, helping to turn around a desperate start to a season which was to end in promotion to Division One. Unfortunately, his progress was halted by knee injuries which threatened to end his career. Several times Tommy returned to full fitness, only to break down in his first match back and, at his lowest ebb, even his team-mates feared he was prepared to quit. Later the situation improved, but Tommy was bitterly hurt by play-off defeat in 2004, and the following year Brian Tinnion stripped him of the captaincy after a spell of poor form. Some supporters demanded his reinstatement, but City's enforcer had reached the end of his tenure in Bristol, and Ian Holloway gave him the chance to relaunch his career at QPR in summer 2005. Amazingly, Tommy sent an open letter to City fans saying how 'gutted' he was with the way things had worked out at the club he loved. Many people at Ashton Gate felt likewise.

BRIAN DRYSDALE

1969/70 — 1976/77

ALAN DICKS never made a wiser investment than the £10,000 that took Brian Drysdale to Ashton Gate in the summer of 1969. The dapper left-back arrived from Hartlepool United as a 26-year-old who had spent his career to date in the League's lower reaches, and to City fans he was an unknown quantity. But they had no cause for concern; Brian settled with aplomb into the role vacated by the long-serving Alec Briggs, not missing a match for more than three seasons and continuing to set high standards of skill and consistency until he was nearly 34.

Amazingly in view of his subsequent achievements, the north-easterner had been released by Lincoln after a handful of appearances and had turned to Hartlepool, his hometown club, to keep him in the game. Prospering under a newly forged managerial alliance – a certain Brian Clough and Peter Taylor – he established a reputation as a polished and dedicated performer, and helped the 'Pool climb out of the Fourth Division for the first time in their history.

Though a few extra inches of stature would have been useful – at 5ft 7in he relied on aerial cover from team-mates – Brian possessed every other attribute essential to a high-class full-back. In defence he was a biting tackler capable of recovering in a trice if a winger slipped past him, he read the game shrewdly and remained calm in moments of crisis. Going forward, he was a speedy raider down the flanks and could use the ball with accuracy and enterprise, particularly with his left foot.

Brian was not noted for his personal assaults on goal, but did enjoy one spectacular success, a wind-assisted 40-yard freak at home to Bolton in September 1974. Such attacking sorties never distracted him from his primary responsibility, and he was as defensively reliable as ever in helping the Robins climb out of the Second Division in 1975/76. But, after 11 games in the top flight, the acquisition of Norman Hunter rendered him surplus to the Robins' requirements. Geoff Merrick was switched to left-back and Brian was left to see out his playing days at Reading, on loan, and Oxford.

Eventually he moved into local amateur football but retained a close interest in the League scene through following the fortunes of his son, Jason, who played for Watford, Swindon and Northampton. Another left-back, Drysdale Jnr strove manfully to reproduce the commitment and efficiency of his father, but could not match his longevity.

BORN: Wingate, Co. Durham, 24.2.43

CITY RECORD:

League: 280 (2) games, 3 goals

FA Cup: 14 games, 0 goals

League Cup: 27 games, 0 goals

Others: 7 games, 1 goal

Total: 328 (2) games, 4 goals

CITY HONOURS:

Promotion from Second Division 75/6

OTHER CLUBS:

Lincoln City 59/60-64/5 (21, 0)

Hartlepool United 65/6-68/9 (170, 2)

Reading on loan 76/7 (16, 0)

Oxford United 77/8 (15, 0)

DARIUSZ 'JACKIE' DZIEKANOWSKI

1991/92 — 1992/93

BRISTOL CITY'S East European enigma was a man misunderstood. The footballing aristocrat brought levels of sophistication never seen before on a regular basis at Ashton Gate. Fans were euphoric, opponents were outclassed and team-mates were inspired. Most of his bosses, however, were just plain exasperated. Jackie was a distinguished Polish international, oozing class and pedigree, but off the field his reputation was rather more primitive.

His arrival in the south-west came as a great shock. Just as the Iron Curtain was crumbling and collapsing in the Soviet Bloc, it seemed chinks were also appearing in the career of Poland's mighty maverick. No one could quite comprehend how City had managed to prise the Polish star away from Celtic. Even Ashton Gate boss Jimmy Lumsden was surprised that the Scottish giants agreed to a modest £255,000 deal, having paid more than twice that to sign him just a few years earlier.

City supporters didn't care, being content to sit back and enjoy one of the most gifted players in their club's history. Jackie's touch was exquisite, his vision sublime and, on song, he would make even his more ordinary team-mates look like they were worthy of the top flight. As the main attraction at an under-achieving club which had always struggled to fulfil its lofty aspirations, Jackie allowed City to dream.

His style, either as an attacking midfielder or a second front-man, was extrovert, full of flourishes and clever little touches which were often too instinctive or far-sighted for some of his colleagues. Meanwhile, off the field, his lifestyle was equally colourful.

Dziekanowski's impact upon arrival was timely for his under-pressure manager. He scored against Southend on his debut before delivering a fabulous performance which was the centrepiece of City's glorious FA Cup victory over Leicester. 'Come On Jackie' the fans were chanting, virtually from day one.

When Lumsden was sacked, the Pole played under Denis Smith, then Russell Osman during an unsettling time for the club. Under Smith he enjoyed himself royally, especially after Andy Cole was signed from Arsenal. Finally Jackie had found a City comrade who could work on his wavelength and in tandem the pair proved a defence's worst nightmare.

But after Osman took over and Cole departed, Jackie appeared to show less interest in football and rather more in Bristol's lively nightlife. He was still a darling of the stands but his performances grew inconsistent. Duly Jackie, real name Dariusz, fell out with Osman and eventually he left, citing homesickness. Such was the fans' displeasure about their hero's exit that they actually booed Osman after he scored for City on the day Dziekanowski left the club.

Latest reports say he is running an electrical business in his native Warsaw. He should be told that, even after all these years, they still talk about him in Bristol, and chuckle with delight.

BORN: Warsaw, Poland, 30.9.62

CITY RECORD:

League: 40 (3) games, 7 goals

FA Cup: 2 games, 2 goals

League Cup: 3 (1) games, 0 goals

Others: 5 (1), 0 goals

Total: 50 (5) games, 9 goals

OTHER CLUBS:

FSO Cars, Widzew Lodz, Legia Warsaw (twice)

Celtic 89/90-91/2 (48, 10)

FC Yverdon, Switzerland, 93/4

FC Cologne, Germany, 94/5

62 Poland caps

ALOUS 'ALEC' EISENTRAGER

1949/50 — 1957/58

IN THE YEARS after the war it took a special kind of courage for a German to build a career in the Football League. Bristol City's Alec Eisentrager – no one in the game called him Alous – not only managed that, but also earned the lasting respect and affection of his team-mates and the Ashton Gate supporters. The circumstances of his nationality, a novelty at first, soon counted for nothing in Bristol, and most opponents and crowds treated him fairly.

In fact, given his talent, it would have been difficult not to warm towards Alec. The diminutive yet muscularly built utility forward, who had been captured on a Dutch airfield as a 16-year-old and spent time in a prisoner-of-war camp before joining first Trowbridge Town and then the Robins, brought with him a catalogue of Continental qualities that seemed a world away from the staple fare of the Third Division South.

Alec was a ball artist whose smooth control, deft flicks and touch of showmanship – his version of the bicycle kick, then something of an innovation in British soccer, was a particularly extravagant party piece – gave a diverting new dimension to the City attack.

Probably he was at his best as a deep-lying schemer, a position that gave full rein to his vision and precise passing ability, and offered frequent opportunities to display his fierce long-range shooting power. On the wing, where manager Pat Beasley often opted to play him, Alec utilised his dribbling and crossing skills to splendid effect, but his lack of pace was sometimes a handicap. He was a firm tackler, quite tough enough to look after himself if challenges became over-physical, but Ernie Peacock and Dennis Roberts were always particularly protective on his behalf.

The majority of Alec's most entertaining performances were given during his first four seasons in Bristol – a four-goal show at home to Newport County in September 1949 was always going to prove hard to top – and his form fell away in the mid-1950s. But after being absent from the side for most of the 1954/55 title campaign, he rallied to show his class in the Second Division before gradually drifting out of first-team contention and returning to non-League football with Merthyr Tydfil.

When he gave up the game, Alec, who had learned to speak perfect English, settled in the Bristol area, where he continued to be held in high regard.

BORN: Hamburg, Germany, 20.7.27

CITY RECORD:

League: 229 games, 47 goals

FA Cup: 11 games, 0 goals

Total: 240 games, 47 goals

BOBBY ETHERIDGE

1956/57 — 1963/64

FUN-LOVING, cocky and blessed with bags of natural talent, Bobby Etheridge was one of the most endearing characters to wear a Robins' shirt since the war. The impish, blond inside-forward cum wing-half was an inventive, silky passer and courageous tackler whose keen foot-balling brain created countless goal opportunities for John Atyeo and company in the late 1950s and early 1960s. With adhesive ball control and exceptional timing in the air to add to his catalogue of qualities, Bobby would surely have progressed to loftier peaks of achievement than was possible with Bristol City but for one frustrating flaw. He was slow, markedly so, and thus his horizons were limited.

Not that the gifted young man whom manager Pat Beasley had signed from Gloucester City in September 1956 and elevated to his Second Division side within three months was discontented with his lot at Ashton Gate. Bobby relished the companionship of his West Country mates and was an all-rounder who threw himself into the local sporting scene. He excelled at everything from darts to county cricket; indeed, as a gifted wicketkeeper he spent 11 years on Gloucestershire's books.

There was even a time, when he was vying with Barrie Meyer in the spring of 1958 to be first choice behind the County Ground stumps, that the summer game might have snatched him away from soccer. But when faced with the choice of touring the South of France with the Robins or battling to build a career in cricket, Bobby chose the Mediterranean option. Thereafter, although he continued as Barrie's understudy, his chance to reach the top in white flannels had gone.

Meanwhile, back on the football field, he was as irrepressible as ever, expert at winding up opponents with his wicked line in patter as well as confounding them with his skills. He was versatile, too, once deputising for Mike Thresher at left-back and cleverly outplaying Fulham winger Graham Leggat. If the Scottish international had used his speed then the City man would have been lost, but Leggat allowed himself to be jockeyed into blind alleys and effectively out of the match.

After leaving Ashton Gate in 1964, Bobby enjoyed a stint with Cheltenham Town before quitting the game. He took up bowls, reached county standard and was still a keen competitor when he died of a heart attack in 1988. All who knew him were devastated by the loss of a lovely man who, right to the end, lived his life to the very full.

BORN: Gloucester, 21.3.34
DIED: Gloucester, 4.4.88

CITY RECORD:

League: 259 games, 42 goals

FA Cup: 23 games, 6 goals

League Cup: 6 games, 1 goal

Others: 2 games, 0 goals

Total: 290 games, 49 goals

BORN: Bristol, 8.5.52

CITY RECORD:

League: 126 (25) games, 32 goals

FA Cup: 9 (1) games, 2 goals

League Cup: 6 (2) games, 1 goal

Others: 2 games, 0 goals

Total: 143 (28) games, 35 goals

CITY HONOURS:

Promotion from Second Division 75/6

OTHER CLUBS:

Hereford United on loan 77/8 (6, 0)

Blackburn Rovers on loan 77/8 (5, 2)

Plymouth Argyle 77/8-79/80 (45, 9)

Brentford on loan 79/80 (8, 2)

Chester 79/80-80/1 (44, 3)

KEITH FEAR

1970/71 — 1976/77

KEITH FEAR was hemmed in by defenders close to the touchline. There seemed to be no danger, and the most the diminutive forward could expect was a throw-in. Suddenly Keith flicked the ball on to his instep, gave a wicked shimmy that threw his chaperons into confusion and, his back to goal, lifted an overhead kick into the path of Chris Garland in the penalty box. The ball was cleared by the Middlesbrough defence, but the chance had been created by an impudent piece of artistry that made the Ashton Gate fans catch their breath.

That incident which lit up a dark December day in 1976 illustrated all that was captivating about a great entertainer who was supremely confident in his own ability. But there was another Keith, the player who could drift frustratingly on the fringe of the action while events took shape around him, and it was he who sometimes loomed largest in the thoughts of Alan Dicks when the manager was picking his team.

It really shouldn't have been a problem at all. In terms of ball skills and vision, Keith was the most gifted City player of the 1970s. Whether playing in midfield, his preferred position, or alongside a big striker, he could turn a game with an incisive pass, an inspired jink or the most delicate of chips, such as the edge-of-the-box effort that caught West Bromwich Albion 'keeper John Osborne a yard off his line at Ashton Gate in February 1975. Despite standing only 5ft 7in, Keith was solidly built and deceptively difficult to dispossess, being adept at shielding the ball before slipping it through the narrowest of openings.

He was, however, short of pace and this, combined with inconsistency and, some would say, a questionable work-rate, prevented him from reaching for the stars. But there were still displays to savour, such as his sparkling contributions in two 1974 FA Cup battles with Leeds. In the first he equalised with a subtle lob, and set up the winner for Donnie Gillies in the Elland Road replay with a glorious through-ball.

Keith, in and out of the side following his 1970 debut, showed some of his most enterprising form in 1976/77, the Robins' first term in the top flight. Sadly, his impetus was halted by a cartilage operation and he opted to try his luck elsewhere. Alan Dicks had not quite pulled off the balancing act of turning Keith into a non-stop chaser without stifling his natural flair, but it had been worth the effort. Without the Fear factor, Bristol City would have been infinitely more predictable – and much less fun.

JOHN GALLEY

1967/68 — 1972/73

JOHN GALLEY was a gangling centre-forward who was short on grace but long on goals. As brave, strong and honest a leader of the line as Ashton Gate has seen, he was majestic in the air and could head the ball harder than many players could kick it. His average of close to a goal every two games, achieved over five years and mostly in times of travail, should have earned him an honoured place in Robins' folk-lore.

Yet John has never really received the credit he deserved for scoring feats which, given their circumstances, make him one of the key figures in the modern history of Bristol City. Twice in the late 1960s his goals averted relegation to the Third Division, and in one of those traumatic campaigns it was probably the Galley scoring touch that prevented manager Alan Dicks – the man destined to lead the club into the top flight during the next decade – from being sacked.

When the ungainly six-footer headed south to complete a £25,000 move from Rotherham in December 1967, his new club was languishing uncomfortably close to the foot of the table, and he hardly looked in shape to inspire a revival. John, who became a City transfer target only after Liverpool had rejected an approach for Alf Arrowsmith, limped into Ashton Gate with a foot in plaster, a victim of tendonitis. But any fears about his fitness were dispelled with a hat-trick at Huddersfield on his debut, and, linking briskly with Chris Garland, he proceeded to give a fair imitation of the Seventh Cavalry.

His 16 goals in 21 games having completed one rescue act, John moved on to the next, scoring heavily in the second half of 1968/69 to remove his manager's head from the chopping block reportedly being made ready. In 1971/72, with the side improving apace, the popular marksman – how the fans loved to chant 'John Ga-llee, John Ga-llee' – became even more prolific, with 22 goals. By then he had worked hard to improve his previously rather basic ball skills, acquiring a competent touch with either foot, and his unselfish approach earned the respect of all who played alongside him.

There seemed no reason why John should not continue to head the Robins' scoring charts for several more seasons, but he accept-ed a £33,000 switch to Nottingham Forest in December 1972. He was never to emulate his Ashton Gate strike-rate elsewhere, however, and he ended up as a centre-half with Hereford United. A rampant poacher had turned game-keeper.

BORN: Clowne, Derbyshire, 7.5.44

CITY RECORD:

League: 172 games, 84 goals

FA Cup: 7 games, 3 goals

League Cup: 16 games, 4 goals

Total: 195 games, 91 goals

OTHER CLUBS:

Wolverhampton Wanderers 62/3-64/5 (5, 2)

Rotherham United 64/5-67/8 (112, 48)

Nottingham Forest 72/3-74/5 (37, 6)

Peterborough United on loan 74/5 (7, 1)

Hereford United 74/5-76/7 (80, 10)

CHRIS GARLAND

1966/67 — 1971/72 & 1976/77 — 1982/83

IT WAS 1966 AND ASHTON GATE was in desperate need of a new hero after the retirement of John Atyeo. Cue Chris Garland, a dashing blond Bristolian with most of the credentials for the vacant post of terrace idol. The young striker had signed professional forms for City in the very month of John's departure, and there was a natural inevitability about his succession as the Robins' star performer.

Chris oozed ability, and, despite a slight deficiency in pace, his future was vibrant with promise. Bounteously endowed with flair and stamina, he was a magnificent athlete, brilliant in the air with a powerful build that enabled him to withstand the most fearsome of challenges. Chris had charisma and the fans fell under its spell, but sheer guts also played an integral part in his game. He was one of the most courageous front-men ever seen at Ashton Gate, throwing himself into challenges most forwards would have shunned; indeed, there are those who reckon that, at times, he was too brave for his own good.

Certainly the Garland style suited John Galley, his partner during his first City stint. Chris was not the most reliable of finishers and not a prolific scorer, but he created so many chances for the lethal John that there were no complaints from manager Alan Dicks. Garland's potential was recognised in 1970 with England under-23 honours, and, with the Robins marooned in the wrong half of the Second Division, a move to the top flight was only a matter of time.

His destination proved to be Stamford Bridge – the fee was £100,000 – and Chris served Chelsea, and subsequently Leicester, with distinction, without quite reaching the predicted heights. Five years later, in 1976, he returned to the City fold, a £110,000 prodigal son charged with the task of helping to retain his first club's hard-won status among the elite.

So much was expected, and, despite a phenomenal work rate, he struggled to make an early impact. Come the crunch, however, Chris produced four goals in as many games, and the Robins survived. Thereafter he was plagued by knee injuries and played only a minor part in the five seasons leading up to the financial trauma of 1982. He was one of eight players who took redundancy, but made a brief comeback in the Fourth Division campaign that followed. When he finally departed, he could look back on a career in which he had played a bold and honourable part in the Ashton Gate story, without being blessed with the best of luck.

In 1992 it was revealed that Chris Garland was suffering from Parkinson's disease, which he has fought with the same exceptional grit that characterised his life in football.

BORN: Bristol, 24.4.49

CITY RECORD:

League: 195 (12) games, 42 goals

FA Cup: 10 (1) games, 3 goals

League Cup: 17 (1) games, 5 goals

Others: 11 games, 3 goals

OTHER CLUBS:

Chelsea 71/2-74/5 (92, 22)

Leicester City 74/5-76/7 (55, 15)

BORN: Baillieston, Lanarkshire, 10.12.63

CITY RECORD:

League: 96 (14) games, 8 goals

FA Cup: 17 games, 1 goal

League Cup: 14 (1) games, 0 goals

Others: 10 games, 1 goal

Total: 137 (15) games, 10 goals

CITY HONOURS:

Promotion from Third Division 89/90

OTHER CLUBS:

Leeds United 82/3-84/5 (30, 3)

Hartlepool United on loan 84/5 (7, 0)

Carlisle United 85/6 (13, 1)

Bolton Wanderers 85/6-86/7 (49, 3)

Rochdale 87/8 (23, 6)

Heart of Midlothian 87/8-88/9 (9, 0)

Watford 90/1 (13, 0)

Exeter City 93/4-95/6 (77, 4)

Scunthorpe United 96/7 (11, 0)

Hartlepool United 97/8 (3, 0)

MARK GAVIN

1988/89 — 1989/90 & 1991/92 — 1993/94

WHEN MARK GAVIN dipped his shoulder, swivelled his hips and set off on his own bewitching variation of the Ali shuffle, the fans could settle back for rare entertainment. That was on a good day. On the other sort, when the muse refused to have anything to do with the stocky Scottish winger, he could be bafflingly anonymous. Ashton Gate regulars could be thankful that, as the successful 1989/90 promotion campaign progressed, Mark was more likely to have them gasping at his trickery than calling for a substitute.

It was not always the case. After making the best possible early impression with a match-winning goal just 85 seconds into his City debut at Gillingham in October 1988, he lapsed into frustrating inconsistency. Mark, a £35,000 acquisition from Hearts, soon became prime target for the boo-boys who had directed their bile at Ralph Milne before his departure for Old Trafford.

Towards the end of the season, however, he began to settle, and showed signs of a productive partnership with newly arrived striker Bob Taylor. Come the following term and Mark at last showed his true form, repeatedly weaving past defenders to reach the byline and cutting back crosses invitingly into the path of incoming colleagues. Though there was still an occasional tendency to over-elaborate, the much-travelled flankman, who had first taken the eye of City supporters as a Bolton player when giving Rob Newman a first-half chasing in the 1986 Freight Rover Trophy Final, was gradually getting the crowd on his side. By the turn of the year, with the championship race hotting up, Mark, equally at home on either wing, was undeniably the side's arch-provider. A typical display came in the home confrontation with Mansfield in April when, oozing confidence, he gulled three defenders and centred for Taylor to head a late equaliser.

The Gavin influence was as strong off the pitch as on it. His extrovert banter and endless quest for tips on the likely outcome of the 3.15 at Wincanton, or whatever contest took his fancy, made for a lively contribution to the dressing room atmosphere. But a parting of the ways became inevitable when manager Joe Jordan refused Mark's wage demands in the summer of 1990, and he joined Watford in exchange for striker Wayne Allison and £100,000.

Gavin didn't linger long at Vicarage Road, being brought back to Ashton Gate by Jimmy Lumsden in a £60,000 deal in December 1991, but his second spell as a Robin proved undistinguished and he moved to Exeter in February 1994.

MIKE GIBSON

1962/63 — 1971/72

'PRETTY STEEP' was how Bristol City manager Fred Ford described the fee he paid for Mike Gibson after signing the chunky young goalkeeper from Shrewsbury Town in the spring of 1963. In fact, Fred was destined to amend his original assessment, with the wry amusement of a man who knew he'd been on the right end of a bargain. Mike went on to become one of the stars – some would say the decisive factor – in the Robins' promotion to the Second Division, and the Ashton Gate boss became more inclined to see his £5,000 outlay as the steal of the century.

Gibson, an England youth international, might not have joined the club at all had not regular custodian Tony Cook been sidelined by injury. Ron Nicholls deputised and the recruit from Gay Meadow was drafted into the reserves, an arrangement that was to be short-lived. By the start of the following season, having worked hard to improve his fitness, Mike was in irresistible form, and quickly claimed the first-team berth he was to fill with distinction for the next eight campaigns.

The newcomer had everything in terms of technique and natural ability, being acrobatic, brave beyond measure and possessed of an inspired sense of timing which told him when to leave his line and when to stand firm. A Gibson speciality was diving full length to save low shots, an Achilles heel of many net-minders, and his success ratio when faced with a lone attacker was phenomenal.

Mike's only flaw was a lack of height, which probably prevented him from attaining First Division or even international status. Standing at 5ft 9in, he was at a grave physical disadvantage against towering strikers, not that his opponents during the 1964/65 climb out of Division Three, and in the subsequent terms in the higher grade, would have noticed any significant deficiency. Often he seemed to form an unbeatable one-man barrier, and a display against Wolves at Molineux in December 1965, when he was constantly bombarded by shots, headers and deflections from every angle, almost redefined the laws of possibility.

In 1972, by now 33, he lost his place to Ray Cashley and moved to Gillingham, before returning to Bristol to become a postman and a youth coach for the Robins. A genial, modest individual, his presence proved a priceless asset to the new generation of Ashton Gate custodians. They could hardly fail to learn from the man whom many describe as the greatest goalkeeper in the history of Bristol City.

BORN: Derby, 15.7.39

CITY RECORD:

League: 332 games, 0 goals

FA Cup: 22 games, 0 goals

League Cup: 22 games, 0 goals

Total: 376 games, 0 goals

CITY HONOURS:

Promotion from Third Division 64/5

OTHER CLUBS:

Shrewsbury Town 60/1-62/3 (76, 0)

Gillingham 72/3-73/4 (80, 0)

DONNIE GILLIES

1972/73 — 1979/80

IT WAS THE MOMENT which kicked off one of the most exciting eras in Bristol City's history. Donnie Gillies was celebrating more than just a giant-killing of seismic proportions when he wheeled away in ecstasy after his second-half winner against mighty Leeds United. The Robins had humbled the nation's most illustrious side, beating them 1-0 in a dramatic FA Cup replay at Elland Road on a wintry February afternoon in 1974, and suddenly the misery of the infamous three-day working week was a little easier to bear for gleeful City fans.

The following morning Donnie picked up a copy of *The Times* newspaper and was shocked to find himself on the front page. It was a moment of national exposure that the Ashton Gate faithful had been yearning for, but the result was to mean more than just 15 minutes of fame for both Donnie and his club.

Boss Alan Dicks, who had been under pressure from the board after some narrow brushes with relegation from the Second Division, was suddenly hailed as a hero and given a long-term deal. Now he was able to build a team that he could rely on to secure promotion – and there were few men more ready for the challenge than Gillies. A man's man prepared to sweat blood for the City shirt, the willing Scot was a feisty and versatile competitor on the pitch, ever ready to charge into battle, and he was always at the head of the queue for a celebration, too.

The moment he slotted home that famous FA Cup goal, after exquisite work from Gerry Gow and Keith Fear, will forever define Donnie

in the memories of supporters, but as far as his manager was concerned, his willingness to play in any position was the quality that most set him apart.

Soon it became apparent that he was as adept at defending as he was at leading the line, and as City began their heroic climb towards the heights of Division One, Donnie was used increasingly as a reliable right-back. While many might have moaned at removal from a glamorous attacking role – another highlight had been notching the winner against Manchester United at Old Trafford in February 1975 – Donnie could not have been happier. He just concentrated on doing his new job well.

Before joining City for £30,000 in March 1973, the former Scotland youth international had excelled for Inverness Clachnacuddin of the Highland League, then top-flight Morton.

He enjoyed seven rollercoaster years at Ashton Gate, but he was devastated by relegation, and when the Robins encountered a cash crisis he caused a stir by moving to Terry Cooper's Bristol Rovers for £50,000 in June 1980. After two seasons at Eastville, he left the League to serve Paulton Rovers, Gloucester City, Bath City, Yeovil Town and Greek side Anorthosis.

Later Donnie continued to live at his family home in Hallatrow while working as a sales representative. In 1990 he was struck by personal tragedy when his wife died, but he fought back and set up a successful fruit and vegetable business. Donnie Gillies never was a man to shirk a challenge.

BORN: Glencoe, Argyllshire, 20.6.51

CITY RECORD:

League: 184 (17) games, 26 goals

FA Cup: 10 (1) games, 1 goal

League Cup: 8 (4) games, 1 goal

Others: 15 (5) games, 2 goals

Total: 217 (27) games, 30 goals

CITY HONOURS:

Promotion from Second Division 75/6

Anglo-Scottish Cup 77/8

OTHER CLUBS:

Morton 71/2-72/3 (47, 23)

Bristol Rovers 80/1-81/2 (59, 0)

SHAUN GOATER

IF BERMUDA CELEBRATES National Shaun Goater Day again, as it did so unforgettably in the year 2000, there is sure to be a generous smattering of Bristol City shirts among the hordes of partygoers. His Ashton Gate spell was brief and ended abruptly, but everyone at the club has fond recollections of the ungainly marksman, whose goals ensured a brief sojourn in the First Division.

Unarguably Shaun was one of the most likeable footballers of the past decade. Indeed, such was his popularity as his career drew towards a close that 'feeding the Goat' became a familiar catchphrase the length and breadth of the land, especially after he was awarded an MBE for his tireless youth work.

Shaun – real name Leonard – had begun a career as a creative midfielder in Bermuda before he was discovered by Manchester United during a tour in 1988. The spindly 18-year-old was on a soccer scholarship at Columbia High School in America at the time, but he packed his bags gleefully and moved to Old Trafford. He failed to make an impact for the Red Devils, though, and switched to Rotherham, where he found his prolific touch in front of goal.

Robins boss Joe Jordan knew he had landed a deadly finisher when he signed Shaun for £175,000 in July 1996. But, as the gangly newcomer ran out of the tunnel for his City debut, fans were not convinced by the man destined to become their talisman. His infectious smile and direct style soon won over the doubters, however, as he delivered an avalanche of goals during two top-scoring campaigns at the club.

Though his nonchalant body language suggested his work-rate could be improved, actually he was a tireless trainer and a truly focused professional. Other aspects of his game were also underrated. As well as being an intuitive poacher, he was strong in the air and awkward to tackle when in full flight – as he demonstrated with one spectacular solo goal against high-flyers Watford at Vicarage Road in 1997/98 – and there were wonderful Ashton Gate hat-tricks against Notts County and Wigan.

Under new boss John Ward, Shaun was at the top of his game as the Robins looked likely to claim the Division Two title in the spring of '98, but the situation turned sour when Manchester City made an approach at a crucial stage of the run-in. Shaun was snatched away for a seemingly paltry £400,000 and the goals dried up for City, who ended up in second place.

At Maine Road Goater's cult status grew and he became a prime icon of the club's revival, initially under another former Bristol City spearhead, Joe Royle. He scored more than a century of goals for the Manchester Blues, and 'The Goat' even bit the hand that first fed him when he notched a brace as City beat bitter local rivals United in the last Maine Road derby.

Since then Shaun has dropped down a level to Reading and has launched various soccer schools and community projects in the Caribbean. Now, they don't bend it like Beckham in Bermuda – they shoot it like Shaun.

BORN: Bermuda, 25.2.70

CITY RECORD:

League: 67 (8) games, 40 goals

FA Cup: 5 games, 0 goals

League Cup: 7 games, 2 goals

Others: 5 (1) games, 1 goal

Total: 84 (9) games, 43 goals

CITY HONOURS:

Promotion from Second Division 97/8

OTHER CLUBS:

Rotherham United 89/90-95/6 (209, 70)

Notts County on loan 93/4 (1, 0)

Manchester City 97/8-02/03 (184, 84)

Reading 03/04-04/05 (43, 12)

Coventry City on loan 04/05 (6, 0)

Bermuda caps

BORN: Glasgow, 29.5.52

CITY RECORD:

League: 368 (7) games, 48 goals

FA Cup: 17 games, 2 goals

League Cup: 27 (2) games, 3 goals

Others: 22 (2) games, 2 goals

Total: 434 (11) games, 55 goals

CITY HONOURS:

Promotion from Second Division 75/6

Anglo-Scottish Cup 77/8

OTHER CLUBS:

Manchester City 80/1-81/2 (26, 5)

Rotherham United 81/2-82/3 (58, 4)

Burnley 83/4 (9, 0)

GERRY GOW

1969/70 — 1980/81

GERRY GOW was once described by Bristol City boss Alan Dicks as something of an ugly duckling, and it might be argued that the abrasive Glaswegian was indeed not the most prepossessing of performers as a youngster. Yet Gerry was to mature into an all-round midfielder who, by the time he left Ashton Gate, was surely the best in town, even if swanlike grace was not exactly a quality that sprang to mind.

Whatever the merits of the Gow style, there is no doubting the enormous contribution he made to the Robins throughout the 1970s. City enjoyed far more possession when the warrior Scot was in their midst, and most of their constructive moves began with Gerry winning the ball. At his peak, when he had added incisive passing skills to the whiplash tackles on which his reputation was based, he was like a scaled-down version of Graeme Souness, admittedly not in the same class but as influential on Dicks's team as Souness was on Bob Paisley's.

Such progress was little short of staggering. The eager teenager who had arrived at Ashton Gate in 1969 had represented a blank footballing canvas, his control rudimentary, his distribution wild. But no one beat him in a 50-50 challenge, and often he came away with the ball when the odds were 70-30 against him. Such fearlessness prompted his manager to blood him in 1970 as a 17-year-old replacement for the experienced Bobby Kellard, and, although at times the combative rookie looked out of his depth, Dicks knew he had a diamond, and persevered.

Gerry, to his credit, worked to improve all aspects of his game, and gradually blossomed into an accomplished player whose part in winning promotion to the First Division in 1976 was inspirational. Perhaps his most rousing display of that period, however, was in subduing Billy Bremner in an epic FA Cup replay victory at Leeds in 1974, and he richly deserved the Scotland under-23 call-up which soon followed.

In the top flight, the Robins' powerhouse stepped up yet another gear, refusing to be cowed by exalted reputations and earning country-wide recognition. When City went down in 1980, it was no surprise when Gerry – just 28 and apparently at the peak of his powers – accepted a move to Manchester City. But, despite some fine showings, he drifted out of contention at Maine Road before finishing his career in the lower divisions and going into non-League management. A nation of midfield opponents could suddenly breathe easier.

IVOR GUY

1945/46 — 1956/57

TO IVOR GUY, surely one of the gentlest and most affable men ever to grace professional sport, football was a simple game. As Bristol City's right-back for 11 seasons, he employed no frills, whenever possible holding firm to his primary tactic of dispatching the ball as far down the field as he could hoof it – and that was a considerable way.

Ivor's claim to fame was the 76-yard free-kick he boomed into the Cardiff City net – without bouncing! – at Ninian Park in October 1945, but there were also many other occasions when his power unlocked defences that had been proof against more subtle methods. His mammoth punts were prone to drop over the heads of startled centre-halves, giving arch-predator John Atyeo, well used to judging the velocity of a Guy missile, the chance to nip behind his markers for a shot at goal.

But the balding defender's chief concern was dealing with marauding wingers, a task he set about in a cool, almost courtly fashion. Although Ivor could tackle when circumstances required, his preferred option was to jockey his opponents towards the touchline, seeming to usher them away from the penalty area with the air of a policeman directing the traffic. He was a tall, strong man who was dominant in the air, but he was not the quickest of movers, being particularly ponderous on the turn. Thus, he and his great friend Jack Bailey, the Robins' small, nippy left-back, formed the most complementary of partnerships.

Ivor's most heroic performance was given not in his customary number-two shirt, but the 'keeper's jersey after Tony Cook was injured in the home clash with Watford during 1954/55, the season in which City became Champions of the Third Division South. Riding his luck he made one fantastic save with his face but displaying creditable resourcefulness and courage, he kept the Hornets at bay to set the scene for Jack Boxley to hit the Robins' late winner.

Almost as vital to the City cause as Ivor's playing merits was his dry wit, which surfaced at the oddest moments. In the heat of the most vital game he might turn to a team-mate and start discussing the previous day's card school. That was typical of an unflappable character whose broad Bristolian tones were sorely missed at Ashton Gate when he retired in 1957 to concentrate on his grocery business in Fishponds. His death after a short illness in 1986 deprived the city of one of the best-loved figures in its sporting history.

BORN: Bristol, 27.2.26

DIED: Bristol, 1.9.86

CITY RECORD:

League: 404 games, 2 goals

FA Cup: 30 games, 1 goal

Total: 434 games, 3 goals

CITY HONOURS:

Third Division South Championship 54/5

NORMAN HUNTER

1976/77 — 1978/79

WHEN NORMAN HUNTER signed a three-year contract with Bristol City shortly before his 33rd birthday in the autumn of 1976, he pledged that he was not moving to Ashton Gate as a soft option in the twilight of his career. He proved to be a man of his word.

The seasoned Leeds United and England warhorse, whose tough image had earned him a niche in British football folklore which his all-round abilities, though considerable, would never have done, was joining a newly promoted side in urgent need of top-level knowhow if it was not to return swiftly to the Second Division. It was a daunting assignment, yet he fulfilled it unflinchingly, not once lowering his standards and giving far more than his experience and professionalism, priceless though they were. Somehow Norman, by his very presence, conferred on the Robins an extra stature and credibility that played a crucial part in their survival among the elite in each of his three terms at the club.

On arrival, after a brief acclimatisation and a booking in his first game, the famous £40,000 recruit was a revelation. It was not Hunter the hard man who took the eye, but Hunter the master footballer, his instinct for doing the right thing at the right time spreading calm assurance through the heart of the City defence. His distribution, particularly with his left foot, was immaculate, and he started countless attacks with shrewd early passes to the front-men. Oh yes, and he could tackle a bit, too, but in truth his reputation bit more legs than he did.

Inevitably, Norman became an instant favourite with the Ashton Gate fans, who basked in the unaccustomed pleasure of watching such a pedigree performer battling in their cause, and the chant of 'Hunter for England', only partly ironic, became a familiar refrain. He made an enormous impression on his teammates, too, being particularly influential in the development of young centre-half Gary Collier.

When his contract was up at the end of the 1978/79 he was offered a two-year extension, though there were those who reckoned he should have been given the chance to become player-boss. In the event, Norman opted to join Allan Clarke as number-two at Barnsley, before embarking on his own surprisingly unsuccessful excursions into management. He left Bristol with his task honourably accomplished, and City's demotion at the end of the following season was a telling comment on his contribution.

BORN: Gateshead, Co. Durham, 29.10.43

CITY RECORD:

League: 108 games, 4 goals

FA Cup: 3 games, 0 goals

League Cup: 2 games, 0 goals

Others: 9 games, 1 goal

Total: 122 games, 5 goals

OTHER CLUBS:

Leeds United 62/3-76/7 (540, 18)

Barnsley 79/80-82/3 (31, 0)

28 England caps (with Leeds United) 1965-74

PFA Footballer of the Year 73/4

MANAGER:

Barnsley 1980-84

Rotherham United 1985-87

BORN: Carluke, Lanarkshire, 15.12.51

CITY RECORD:

League: 38 (19) games, 8 goals

FA Cup: 1 (1) games, 0 goals

League Cup: 7 (1) games, 0 goals

Others: 7 (4) games, 4 goals

Total: 53 (25) games, 12 goals

CITY HONOURS:

Freight Rover Trophy Finalist 86/7

OTHER CLUBS:

Morton 68/9-70/1 (12, 2)

Leeds United 71/2-77/8 (169, 35)

Manchester United 77/8-80/1 (109, 37)

AC Milan 81/2-82/3 (52, 2)

Verona 83/4 (12, 1)

Southampton 84/5-86/7 (48, 12)

52 Scotland caps 1972–82

MANAGER:

Bristol City 1988-90

Heart of Midlothian 1990-93

Stoke City 1993-94

Bristol City 1994-97

JOE JORDAN

1986/87 — 1989/90

WHEN HE WAS KICKED in the teeth, he came back for more. Joe Jordan's career, as manager and player, thrived on simplicity. A product of tough Scottish stock, he valued sheer determination and honesty, and it helped him to mighty achievements in a footballing life which took in spells at Leeds, Manchester United and AC Milan, as well as World Cup action for his country. Yet for all those high-flying exploits, few of Jordan's clubs benefited more from his old-fashioned approach than Bristol City in 1989/90.

Joe is a humble, sincere and essentially friendly man. But also he can be obstructive and confrontational, as numerous City players, and football reporters, discovered to their misfortune during his two reigns at Ashton Gate. Some found his disciplined regime overwhelming, but this was no firebrand dictator, merely a straight fellow who wanted his players to show the same willingness to strain every sinew as he always did himself.

During his teenage years, the left-sided attacker carved out a career as a draughtsman while playing for Scottish minnows Morton. But when Leeds United sent a scout to look at his team-mate Gerry Sweeney, it was Big Joe who caught the eye. During one of his first appearances in a Leeds shirt he lost his front teeth, a collison with goalkeeper Bill Glazier in a reserve match at Coventry giving him that famous gap-toothed scowl. He featured in the Yorkshiremen's 1973/74 League Championship triumph before joining the Red Devils in 1978.

After a lucrative spell in Italy, Jordan arrived at Ashton Gate via Southampton. He was in his middle thirties, his playing prime clearly behind him, but he was warmly received in Bristol, where his appetite for tireless graft was admired. In 1988 Joe succeeded Terry Cooper as player-boss and swiftly instilled a more rigorous approach, using his star-studded contacts book to make shrewd signings, including Bob Taylor of Leeds. The rookie manager proved to be an inspiration, and plotted City's progress to the 1989 League Cup semi-finals, where they were narrowly defeated by Brian Clough's Nottingham Forest.

In the following campaign, Joe delivered promotion. Spearheaded by the prolific Taylor, City amassed 91 points but had to be content with the Division Three runners-up spot after being leapfrogged by Bristol Rovers following a dramatic 3-0 derby defeat at Twerton Park. A season later Joe was head-hunted by Hearts, and then took over at Stoke before returning to City for a three-year stint in the mid 1990s. This time his progress was overshadowed by uncertainties over the board's future and the second tenure proved unfulfilling, with a series of mid-table finishes.

In 2004/05 the gruesome fangs were no longer on show, but Jordan was still in love with football, enjoying an Indian summer coaching at Portsmouth. His sons, Andrew and Tom, made the grade as professionals and both spent time at City. They could not have wished for a finer role model than their dad.

BORN: DR Congo, 28.12.84

CITY RECORD:

League: 44 (41) games, 31 goals

FA Cup: 1 (4) games, 3 goals

League Cup: 2 (1) games, 2 goals

Others: 4 (3) games, 2 goals

Total: 51 (49) games, 38 goals

OTHER CLUBS:

Reading 05/06-

LEROY LITA

THOSE WHO BELIEVE FOOTBALLERS have the easy life should meet Leroy Lita. The notion of triumphing over adversity barely covers the astounding progress of the precociously talented marksman, hailed as a goal-scoring sensation after only one full season as a first-team regular at Ashton Gate. The lad bubbles with self-belief but is mercifully free of arrogance, an attractive attitude born, perhaps, from his traumatic origins in war-torn central Africa.

Leroy's mum had only one wish when her son was born; for him to move away from the hellish conditions of Congo. She never dared to hope that one day he would be on course to enjoy all the trappings that go with being one of the most exciting young stars outside the Premiership.

When the Litas moved to the UK in the early 1990s, they had nothing. But Leroy was prepared to give everything to achieve his dream. Duly his tenacious approach and deadly eye for goal on the parks of London was spotted by Chelsea. He joined the Stamford Bridge giant's academy but felt that his chances were limited at a club which was increasingly looking abroad for players, even for their youth team.

He searched elsewhere, having trials with a handful of top-flight clubs and also Bristol Rovers. But when he witnessed the impressive youth set-up at City he was quick to sign on. At the time few clubs in the country were producing as much home-grown talent as the Robins and, under the guidance of academy director Tony Fawthrop, Leroy flourished.

In 2002/03 he broke into the first team as a 17-year-old and scored a last-minute goal at Port Vale which secured three points. His bouncing, effervescent style was welcomed instantly by the supporters, who were quick to welcome him as the predator the club so desperately needed.

Boss Danny Wilson was more cautious, however, and for two seasons Leroy was consigned to the substitutes' bench. City fans were dismayed and outraged when the boy was not even among the replacements for the 2004 play-off final which ended in disastrous defeat against Brighton. That day City lacked the zest and firepower which Leroy might have provided, and his absence appeared inexplicable. Shortly afterwards Wilson was fired and his successor, Brian Tinnion, was never to make the same mistake.

Tinnion and Lita struck a deal when the new manager was sworn in. In return for the squad number eight, Leroy promised to deliver 20 goals – which he had done by January. As City's first-choice front-man, he was the leading scorer by a country mile, and he struck up a fruitful partnership with Steve Brooker.

After he netted on his debut for the England under-21 side, his market value soared, making him the club's most valuable asset, so it was no surprise when he joined Reading in July 2005 for £1 million plus an undisclosed sell-on percentage. If anyone at Bristol City had the right ingredients to make it all the way to the top, then clearly it was Leroy Lita. Should he go on to scale that ultimate pinnacle, then no one would appreciate it more than the amiable Congolese.

ANDY LLEWELLYN

1982/83 — 1993/94

ANDY LLEWELLYN never saw the need to over-complicate life. He was a rare gem of stability in uncertain times for Bristol City. Brought up within a trademark punt of Ashton Gate, the stocky right-back had his feet firmly on the ground and knew exactly how to play to his strengths.

Affable Andy was a consummate professional who made close on 400 senior appearances for the Robins, yet a typical game might pass with the fans barely noticing he was on the pitch. That was not because he was unproductive; rather that he was a monument to unobtrusive efficiency, the type who could play for 90 minutes without putting a foot wrong.

The Llewellyn game was basic, disciplined and effective. In an era when attacking full-backs were becoming commonplace, Andy's clear priority was to defend. His method was to get a foot in before attackers could even blink and then leave the flashier stuff to the likes of fellow defenders Martin Scott and Rob Newman.

Successive managers knew what they would get from the loyal Bristolian and it is to his credit that he was regularly one of the first names on the teamsheet for Terry Cooper, Joe Jordan, Jimmy Lumsden and Denis Smith during his 12 years at the club.

As a boy he attended The Chase School in Mangotsfield, where he was viewed as an exceptional prospect and he was capped several times by England at youth level. City were delighted to sign him on as a trainee and, despite his relatively short stature, he was fast-tracked into the first team within just five months.

Andy was only 16 when Cooper gave him his League debut at Rochdale in December 1982. Linking smoothly with more experienced performers such as Brian Williams, John Bailey and Newman, he matured with distinction and soon he emerged as a Robins mainstay. He was part of the side that suffered penalty shoot-out defeat by Mansfield in the Freight Rover Trophy Final at Wembley in 1987, and missed reaching the Third Division play-offs by one point.

But Llewellyn's finest times as a Robin arrived at the turn of the decade. Having starred in City's memorable FA Cup victory against Chelsea, he featured in every game as promotion was clinched in 1989/90, and in the following term his dependability won widespread admiration as he was voted player of the year as City consolidated their place in Division Two.

Andy was still on duty as Liverpool were ejected from the FA Cup in 1994, but that proved to be something of a swansong for one of the club's most loyal servants. After linking up with Cooper for a brief loan spell at Exeter, he was sold to Yeovil by Russell Osman, then wound down his playing days at Bishop Sutton and Weston-super-Mare before managing Clevedon United.

Eminently enthusiastic about the game, Llewellyn remains one of the most popular members of the local footballing community.

BORN: Bristol, 26.2.66

CITY RECORD:

League: 296 (12) games, 3 goals

FA Cup: 23 games, 0 goals

League Cup: 20 games, 0 goals

Others: 28 (2) games, 0 goals

Total: 367 (14) games, 3 goals

CITY HONOURS:

Promotion from Third Division 89/90

Freight Rover Trophy Finalist 86/7

OTHER CLUBS:

Exeter City on loan 93/4 (15, 0)

Hereford United 94/5 (4, 0)

BORN: Aberdeen, 11.7.40

CITY RECORD:

League: 203 (2) games, 12 goals

FA Cup: 15 games, 2 goals

League Cup: 6 games, 0 goals

Total: 224 (2) games, 14 goals

CITY HONOURS:

Promotion from Third Division 64/5

OTHER CLUBS:

Huddersfield Town 57/8-60/1 (67, 6)

Stockport County 68/9-69/70 (64, 1)

Crewe Alexandra 70/1 (5, 0)

GORDON LOW

LOFTY LEFT-HALF Gordon Low, the man who succeeded John Atyeo as captain of Bristol City, was always more popular with his team-mates than with the fans. His was an unspectacular contribution to the side, neither breathtakingly skilful nor rousingly spirited, and in terms of terrace popularity he suffered for it.

Robins boss Fred Ford plucked the powerful but rather ponderous Scot from Huddersfield Town reserves for £3,000 in March 1961, just five months after snapping up Jack Connor from the same source. Gordon, who as a schoolfriend of Denis Law had followed the brilliant inside-forward to the Yorkshire club, established himself steadily at Ashton Gate, making several early appearances as Jack's deputy at centre-half.

His City future, however, was to lie in the number-six shirt, which he inherited from Irishman Tom Casey in 1963. On gaining a regular place, Gordon showed efficiency in the air and control on the ground, but the most impressive aspect of the Low game was his ability to spray long, raking passes with his left foot. A crisp striker of the ball, he had a happy knack of picking out the head of Atyeo from free-kicks. He also scored the occasional long-range goal, such as his rasping 25-yard cross-shot against Queen's Park Rangers at Loftus Road in December 1963.

Against that, Gordon was slow, and, although he could tackle firmly enough, it was not with the ferocity usually associated with wing-halves from north of the border. Thus, while he could look a useful performer when the Robins were controlling a game, he lacked the crowd appeal of, say, the battling Connor if City had a fight on their hands.

Nevertheless Gordon, an enthusiastic on-the-field organiser, was an ever-present in both the 1964/65 Third Division promotion season and the following term, in which the Robins finished fifth in Division Two. He was named as skipper for 1966/67 but, sadly, City's performances and his personal displays fell away, and the action sometimes seemed to pass him by as he strove in vain to inspire his team-mates.

When Alan Dicks took over as manager Gordon was ousted from both the captaincy and the side, and he slipped away to complete his playing days in the lower divisions. The fans had never warmed to him, which was their prerogative, but those who spent so much time on his back might now reflect that they offered little encouragement to an honest professional when he most needed their help.

KEVIN MABBUTT

1977/78 — 1981/82

DROP THE NAME OF KEVIN MABBUTT into any conversation on Bristol football and the reaction is sadly predictable. Talk turns immediately to the absurd attempt to promote the diminutive striker as a soccer superstar before he had earned the status where it mattered – on the field. And that is a shame, because although Kevin was never likely to reach the very highest class, he was a talented prospect who, despite his flashy image, was utterly dedicated to the game.

He had been destined to become a professional footballer since early childhood. His father Ray, the long-serving Bristol Rovers wing-half, had worked diligently to prepare his two sons for League careers, and both Kevin and his younger brother Gary had responded enthusiastically. Always the more naturally talented of the two, the older boy made rapid progress in the Pirates' youth sides and there was tremendous disappointment at Eastville when he opted to sign for City.

At Ashton Gate Kevin was always the-lad-most-likely-to, a gleeful jack-in-the-box of a goal-scorer blessed with speed, skill and bags of confidence. He made his debut as an 18-year-old in August 1977 and enjoyed a perkily promising early run in the team, but it was in the following season, when his appearances became increasingly frequent, that he shot to national prominence with a cheeky opportunist hat-trick at Old Trafford. That day United's Scottish internationals Martin Buchan and Gordon McQueen had no answer to his darting, diagonal excursions into the penalty box and, combining effectively with big Joe Royle, he wreaked havoc.

But while Kevin's career was gathering momentum nicely, his publicity machine was moving even faster. With his white Lotus emblazoned with his personal slogan and other jet-set trappings, he became the target of sneers and jealousy, doing himself no favours as a young man still learning his trade. All the while, it must be stressed, he maintained the work-rate that is the Mabbutt family trademark, and to this day he is held up by his former coaches as a shining example to youngsters.

But, with City plummeting from First Division to Third, the ambitious Kevin understandably sought fresh impetus, and moved to Crystal Palace in exchange for £100,000 and defender Terry Boyle. After an encouraging first term at Selhurst Park he was bedevilled by knee and pelvic injuries, and ultimately forced to quit. A road which so many had predicted would lead to stardom had ended in desperate disappointment.

BORN: Bristol, 5.12.58

CITY RECORD:

League: 112 (17) games, 29 goals

FA Cup: 8 games, 7 goals

League Cup: 12 games, 3 goals

Others: 18 (1) games, 8 goals

Total: 150 (18) games, 47 goals

CITY HONOURS:

Anglo-Scottish Cup 77/8

OTHER CLUBS:

Crystal Palace 81/2-84/5 (75, 22)

BORN: Goole, Yorkshire, 15.12.52

CITY RECORD:

League: 205 (26) games, 31 goals

FA Cup: 10 (2) games, 4 goals

League Cup: 15 games, 2 goals

Others: 22 (3) games, 9 goals

Total: 252 (31) games, 46 goals

CITY HONOURS:

Promotion from Second Division 75/6

Anglo-Scottish Cup 77/8

OTHER CLUBS:

Leeds United 71/2-72/3 (2, 0)

Barnsley 81/2-82/3 (15, 0)

Scunthorpe United 82/3 (2, 0)

Doncaster Rovers 82/3 (13, 0)

JIMMY MANN

1974/75 — 1981/82

JIMMY MANN confessed he could not hit a barn door from five yards out . . . but he could smash one off its hinges from 40! The modest Yorkshireman never was a man to stand on ceremony, and in September 1979 he proved it in some style. With European Champions Nottingham Forest set to visit Ashton Gate, City were under strict orders from manager Alan Dicks to keep a tight and orderly ship. But on the day, Jimmy let loose.

In a moment of gloriously mad inspiration, he skipped past several midfielders before unleashing the most venomous shot that City fans had ever seen. Forest's England 'keeper Peter Shilton was in his pomp at the time, but there was absolutely nothing he could do about the 35-yard thunderbolt which whistled into the top left corner of his net as the East Stand erupted in euphoria. The season ended in relegation as the club stared down the barrel at possible bankruptcy, but at least Jimmy's flash of genius had provided supporters with one of the most spectacular goals south Bristol had ever witnessed.

Mann was born and bred in the Yorkshire Dales, so his family was as proud as punch when he was offered schoolboy terms, leading to a professional contract at Leeds United in 1969. But his spell with his local club was largely miserable as the midfielder struggled to make headway into Don Revie's team of world-beaters. Still, when City approached him about a move south in 1974 he was initially reluctant, but eventually he signed when he discovered that John Shaw was part of the deal. That free transfer was to prove the making of Jimmy.

A friendly, down-to-earth fellow and a keen fisherman, he was popular among City players and soon he became a key factor in one of the most successful eras in the club's history. Pretty quickly he earned a national reputation through his knack of producing the spectacular, his blistering long-range howitzers from free play and his expertise at free-kicks contributing significantly to City's long-awaited return to the top flight in 1976. The following season, he was equally impressive and was a prominent figure as the Anglo-Scottish Cup was lifted in 1977/78.

Jimmy remained loyal to the cause, but following relegation his wages became a burden on the crisis-torn club's bank balance. He stuck with the Robins as they plummeted to the Third Division, but with creditors hammering at the doors in 1981 his days were numbered. Thus he became one of the Ashton Gate Eight, whose contracts were terminated in a bid to keep the club alive.

After he was asked to make himself redundant, his family's welfare was on the line, but he was rescued by a former City comrade. Norman Hunter had taken charge at Barnsley and swiftly offered Jimmy a chance to relaunch his career and move back home in the process. He went on to spells at Scunthorpe, Doncaster, Goole Town and Bentley Victoria, then worked as a jobbing security guard and a milkman back in his birthplace of Goole.

BORN: Bristol, 29.4.51

CITY RECORD:

League: 361 (6) games, 10 goals

FA Cup: 16 (1) games, 2 goals

League Cup: 30 games, 1 goal

Others: 20 games, 0 goals

Total: 427 (7) games, 13 goals

CITY HONOURS:

Promotion from Second Division 75/6

Anglo-Scottish Cup 77/8

GEOFF MERRICK

1967/68 — 1981/82

GEOFF MERRICK in an Arsenal shirt? It would have been unthinkable to the legions of Ashton Gate supporters who saw their skipper and defensive kingpin as indispensable to the City cause. Yet there are those who swear that, had the home-loving Bristolian moved to Highbury when the Gunners inquired about him in the mid-1970s, he would have gone on to play for England. Others maintain that he reached his full potential with his only professional club, and need have no regrets about what might have been.

Either way, there is no disputing the immense contribution Geoff made to the Robins from the time he made his debut as a 17-year-old in 1968 until that emotional day, nearly 14 years later, when he helped ensure their very survival by accepting reduced redundancy money as one of the Ashton Gate Eight.

An England schoolboy international wing-half, Geoff had always been expected to make the grade, but his progress as a teenage professional was delayed by niggling injuries, and it was not until 1971/72 that he managed a settled sequence of senior outings. During that term, in which he partnered two big stoppers, first Dickie Rooks and then David Rodgers, in the middle of the back four, he became City captain at the age of 20, a mark of his maturity and impeccable temperament.

Geoff, a left-footer, was blessed with nearly every asset demanded of the model centre-back. He was fast, tackled powerfully and precisely, was brilliant in the air despite standing only 5ft 9in, and had a finely honed positional sense. The only drawback, all that stopped him from walking into his country's team no matter what club's shirt was on his back, was a tendency to lack accuracy in his distribution.

In general, though, he was superb, his quietly effective leadership and commanding personal form setting the loftiest of standards for his team-mates throughout the 1975/76 promotion campaign. But two months into City's first term in the top flight, Geoff received a severe jolt. Norman Hunter was signed and the skipper was consigned to left-back, a role in which he was efficient but not outstanding. When Norman departed three years later, Geoff reclaimed his preferred position, but despite showing all his old authority, he could do little to halt the Robins' slide down the divisions. That rapid decline, and the financial emergency that followed, led the Merrick career to a frustrating close. For such a magnificent servant of Bristol City, it was not a fitting farewell.

BORN: Aberdeen, 26.5.74

CITY RECORD:

League: 229 (44) games, 54 goals

FA Cup: 15 (1) games, 7 goals

League Cup: 12 (3) games, 0 goals

Others: 21 (5) games, 8 goals

Total: 277 (53) games, 69 goals

CITY HONOURS:

Promotion from Second Division 97/8

LDV Vans Trophy 02/03

Auto Windscreens Shield Finalist 99/00

OTHER CLUBS:

Aston Villa 95/6-96/7 (4, 0)

Reading 03/04 (34, 5)

SCOTT MURRAY

CITY FANS had got it wrong – size, after all, did not matter. An air of scepticism had immersed the Red half of Bristol when it emerged that pint-sized Scott Murray was making his way down the M5 from Aston Villa. With the likes of Junior Bent and Greg Goodridge firmly etched in Ashton Gate memories, the prospect of another vertically challenged wide-man hardly inspired supporters to drool in anticipation.

Little did they know that they were about to welcome their most exciting match-winner in years. Scott was never one to waste time and his boundless determination and unwavering enthusiasm ensured he soon became the darling of the stands, even among those south Bristol critics most disposed to carp.

Like Bent and Goodridge, Murray was endowed with searing pace and an assured touch, which enabled him to glide past defenders; however, Scott possessed the vital ingredient that his predecessors lacked – he could score goals. All too often those other tiny wingers would leave the crowd howling in exasperation after ballooning over from four yards, but Scott could create his own chances and often convert them more surely than the strikers.

The Aberdeen-born flier was spotted playing for Highland League Fraserburgh by Ron Atkinson, who promptly offered him a deal at Villa Park. Murray was both thrilled and shocked by the invitation and it sums up his down-to-earth attitude that he insisted on working out his notice in his job as a fork-lift driver before moving to the Midlands. In the event, he struggled to gain regular football at Villa and was snapped up by John Ward midway through 1997/98 to reinforce Bristol City's tilt at promotion from Division Two.

Murray's jovial character ensured that he became a popular member of the squad, always at the heart of dressing-room banter, and on the pitch he improved with every passing season, so that by 2002/03 he was truly breathtaking. Playing mainly at right wing-back, Scott terrorised Second Division defenders, his relentless running and keen eye for the net taking him to the top of City's scoring charts with 26 goals. Not surprisingly, by the summer his agent was inundated with approaches from leading clubs.

Come July he opted for Reading in a £650,000 deal which many felt didn't reflect his wealth of talent. Still, Scott's tenure at the Madejski Stadium began promisingly, but as pangs of homesickness grew ever stronger, life became unaccustomedly strained for the normally easy-going 29-year-old. His return to City, barely nine months after his departure, was hailed as the ultimate boost to Danny Wilson's promotion push. But the pressure on the Aberdonian was immense and he struggled with form and fitness as the Robins lost their grip on the top two and ultimately crashed out in the play-off final.

Happily a much-needed rest over the close-season rejuvenated Scott, and he was handed the club captaincy by new manager Brian Tinnion. It would take more than a few bad games to take the steam out of the flying Scotsman.

ROB NEWMAN

1981/82 — 1990/91

BEGGING BRYAN ROBSON'S PARDON, Bristol City had their own Captain Marvel. He played at full-back, centre-half, midfield and even up front, he served the Robins through good times and bad, and Ashton Gate fans of his era could barely imagine the place without him. Invariably he wore the biggest grin in football and, if pressed, answered to the name of 'Biff'. But most people knew him as Rob Newman, one of the most accomplished all-round performers outside the top flight throughout his decade in south Bristol.

Yet Rob, who had amassed close on 500 senior appearances for City by the time of his £600,000 move to Norwich in July 1991, once came agonisingly close to rejection. When manager Alan Dicks sat down to draw up a list of prospective apprentices, he wrote down ten names and then pondered. Almost as an afterthought, he scribbled an 11th, that of Rob Newman.

Not very much later, the young Wiltshireman was pitchforked into the Third Division relegation scrap in the traumatic aftermath of the Ashton Gate Eight's departure in February 1982. Many careers withered in their infancy – none of the ten others who joined up with Rob made the grade – and the Robins duly went down.

He survived, playing most of his early games at right-back, though many observers reckoned he was most effective as a buccaneering midfielder. After helping City rise from the Fourth in 1984, Rob suffered a broken leg followed by a loss of form, and this was a period when his ability to fill almost any role stood him in good stead.

It was a lull from which he bounced back quickly – never has there been a more enthusiastic footballer – ultimately becoming skipper and settling imperiously into the position of central defender from which he led City back to Division Two in 1990. His cultured passing, coolness and vision more than made up for a marginal lack of pace, though at 6ft 2in he could perhaps have been more dominant in the air.

In attack, often Rob proved a devastating reinforcement. His 25-yard free-kick at home to Chester in January 1990 was a classic of its kind, though perhaps his finest hour in front of goal came in May 1983 against Crewe when, with City one down after 75 minutes, he was switched from full-back to striker and netted twice to win the match.

From a Robins viewpoint it was a shame that Rob departed for Carrow Road while still in his pomp, but his desire to test himself in the top division was entirely understandable. He went on to serve the Canaries nobly throughout most of the 1990s, but always remained one of Ashton Gate's favourite sons, and a shoe-in to any list of Bristol City's finest ever footballers.

BORN: Bradford-on-Avon, Wiltshire, 13.12.63

CITY RECORD:

League: 382 (12) games, 52 goals

FA Cup: 27 games, 2 goals

League Cup: 29 (1) games, 2 goals

Others: 33 games, 5 goals

Total: 471 (13) games, 61 goals

CITY HONOURS

Promotion from Fourth Division 83/4

Promotion from Third Division 89/90

Freight Rover Trophy 85/6

Freight Rover Trophy Finalist 86/7

OTHER CLUBS:

Norwich City 91/2-97/8 (205, 14)

Motherwell on loan 97/8 (11, 0)

Wigan Athletic on loan 97/8 (8, 0)

Southend United 98/9-01/02 (72, 11)

MANAGER:

Southend 2001-03

Cambridge United 2005-

BORN: Bristol, 6.12.38

CITY RECORD:

League: 281 (6) games, 4 goals

FA Cup: 19 games, 0 goals

League Cup: 20 games, 0 goals

Total: 320 (6) games, 4 goals

CITY HONOURS:

Promotion from Third Division 64/5

OTHER CLUBS:

Waterford, Republic of Ireland, 72/3

GORDON PARR

SOMEHOW IT CAME AS A SURPRISE. Gordon Parr, after 15 combative years of making life as uncomfortable as possible for Bristol City's opponents, was embarking on his first campaign in the European Cup. The swarthy six-footer, a wing-half cum central defender noted for power and pace rather than the finer points of the game, had been released by Ashton Gate boss Alan Dicks in the spring of 1972 and joined Waterford, who had qualified for the Continent's premier club competition as Irish champions. The adventure didn't last long, a first-round knockout putting paid to dreams of meeting the likes of Cruyff and company, but it had been a rewarding finale to a worthy if commonplace career.

There had never been anything fancy about Gordon's football. Always supremely fit – he embarrassed senior players in the late 1950s by leaving them standing on training runs – he made his debut as an attacking right-half who chased all over the pitch to very little effect. After a lengthy spell in the reserves he was recalled in 1962 by manager Fred Ford, and having adopted a steadier approach, he became a reliable marker, adept at stopping more creative players from expressing themselves.

Gordon played his part in a solid start to the successful 1964/65 Third Division promotion campaign before being replaced by Chuck Drury, and it seemed that one of the Robins' most fearsome tacklers since the war might be on his way out. But Gordon showed resilience, returning to the side and ultimately evolving into a more impressive performer alongside Jack Connor at centre-back than he had ever been in his former role.

He gave yeoman service throughout the annual late-1960s relegation struggles, and also distinguished himself in cup confrontations with loftier opposition. Two of Gordon's doughtiest displays came in the 1970/71 League Cup semi-final against Spurs, in which he was unsettled by neither the wily Alan Gilzean nor the forceful Martin Chivers, and City failed to reach Wembley only after extra time in the second leg.

The steadfast Bristolian eventually bowed to the youthful challenge of Geoff Merrick, departing for his Waterford interlude before enjoying two seasons with Western League Minehead. When he gave up the game to concentrate on his work as an electrical contractor, Gordon could be content that he had made the utmost use of limited natural talent, and that never in his life had he let his side down.

BORN: Bristol, 11.12.24

DIED: Bristol, 12.2.73

CITY RECORD:

League: 343 games, 7 goals

FA Cup: 14 games, 1 goal

Total: 357 games, 8 goals

CITY HONOURS:

Third Division South Championship 54/5

ERNIE PEACOCK

1946/47 — 1958/59

NEVER DID SUCH A CHANGE come over any man as the one that transformed Ernie Peacock when he walked out to play for Bristol City. Gone was the gentle, quietly spoken individual who had arrived at the ground before the match; in his place was a flame-haired gladiator breathing fire and brimstone, ready to take on the world in the name of his beloved Robins.

Ernie was a ball-winning defensive wing-half who was not happy unless he was in the thick of every piece of action. At times he would charge around the pitch like a man possessed, tackling, harassing and generally imposing his will on the opposition. Tales of his confrontations have passed into Ashton Gate legend, none more so than the mid-1950s dust-up with his equally passionate Eastville counterpart, Jackie Pitt, which resulted in a double sending-off.

When City played Rovers, Ernie went to war with awesome commitment, but he was a lovely man who never bore a grudge, and minutes after that particularly stormy tussle the two fighting cocks were laughing together and looking forward to the next time.

The Peacock approach often made him a target for abuse at away matches, and Millwall fans always seemed to reserve some vintage vitriol for the Robins' dynamo. At the end of one ferocious encounter at the Den he was denounced colourfully by a large group of Lions supporters, and team-mates swear that he was ready to take on the lot of them single-handed. Ernie, who frequently played at centre-half after the retirement of Dennis Roberts in 1954, was almost as fearsome in training as he was in the most vital of matches, utterly refusing to admit defeat. He was known to dive full-length to head goals in five-a-side sessions on tarmac, grazing himself hideously but not even pausing to wipe away the blood before getting up to continue the game.

He was never a creative player, his distribution not being in the same class as his work-rate, but throughout most of the 1950s a City side without Ernie, whether before or after promotion to the Second Division, would have been unimaginable. After leaving Ashton Gate in 1959 he lent his enthusiasm to Southern League Weymouth and became a successful car salesman before his life was claimed by a heart attack at the age of 48. His memory, however, will survive as long as the Robins themselves. And, no matter what the future holds for Bristol City, one thing is certain; no one will ever wear that red shirt with greater pride than Ernie Peacock.

BORN: Bath, Somerset, 6.5.78

CITY RECORD:

League: 237 (1) games, 0 goals

FA Cup: 16 games, 0 goals

League Cup: 11 games, 0 goals

Others: 22 games, 0 goals

Total: 286 (1) games, 0 goals

CITY HONOURS:

LDV Vans Trophy 2002/03

STEVE PHILLIPS

1998/99 —

STEVE PHILLIPS is living proof that no young footballer should ever stop dreaming. Some spend all their lives honing their trade, but City's number-one was given just a few weeks to graduate from non-league nobody to polished professional.

It was a tall order for a 19-year-old plucked from the obscurity of his home-town club, Paulton Rovers. But the Bath-born lad took it all in his stride and within a mere 12 months he had swapped comparatively sleepy Saturdays in the Dr Martens' League for the seething cauldron of life in the First Division.

In an era where clubs tend not to look at triallists past the age of 14, old-fashioned Steve had bucked the trend. He may have been a late starter but he became one of City's greatest assets.

For most Ashton Gate followers with a sense of history, Mike Gibson is the outstanding City 'keeper of the post-war years, so it was fitting that he should be one of the major influences on Steve's progress from raw but promising displays for Paulton Rovers reserves. It's a tad ironic, though, that thanks partly to Mike's splendid coaching skills, eventually Steve would challenge him for the mantle of the Robins' top custodian of the last half a century.

Phillips was thrust dramatically into the first team as City swept to a rare victory under Benny Lennartsson's guidance, prevailing 2-0 in a home encounter with Sheffield United in December 1998.

The youngster was sweating over his future at the time, having been shipped out on loan to Evesham, but after his starring debut he kept his place for 15 games. The following season was rocky under new boss Tony Pulis, and the 'keeper found himself battling for a place with Billy Mercer and, later, Mike Stowell. In 2002 he emerged triumphant when Danny Wilson made him the top man.

Steve's reputation for athleticism and gravity-defying shot-stopping soared during the next two seasons as the club twice finished third and narrowly missed out on promotion each time. In 2003/04 he saw just 37 goals go past him – the best record in the Second Division – and he was named in the prestigious Team of the Year by his fellow professionals.

The following season proved slightly more difficult as new manager Brian Tinnion rang the changes in defence, but still Phillips turned in some admirable displays. For example, in one League Cup clash with Everton he made a string of stellar saves against James McFadden, which earned national recognition.

Since bursting on the League scene, Steve has been linked with several Premiership clubs, but he is a West Countryman through and through. For a fellow who left Paulton Rovers only reluctantly, it was always going to need one special offer to lure him to the bright lights of the top flight. The flashy cars might line his drive, but Steve Phillips remains a confirmed country boy at heart.

BORN: Glasgow, 28.6.35

DIED: Nottingham, 30.11.04

CITY RECORD:

League: 66 games, 7 goals

FA Cup: 9 games, 0 goals

Total: 75 games, 7 goals

OTHER CLUBS:

Nottingham Forest 57/8-64/5 (236, 51)

Huddersfield Town 64/5-66/7 (65, 4)

Mansfield Town 68/9-70/1 (104, 2)

JOHN QUIGLEY

1966/67 — 1967/68

JOHN QUIGLEY was the perfect prescription for a Bristol City side that was looking ominously off-colour in the autumn of 1966. After winning promotion from the Third Division 18 months earlier the Robins had enjoyed an enterprising first season back in the higher grade, but then began to struggle alarmingly. Manager Fred Ford, deprived of his senior professional by the recent retirement of John Atyeo, decided that an injection of experience and stability was needed, and administered it in the form of the wiry little 31-year-old Glaswegian.

The Quigley services did not come cheaply, Fred parting with popular, locally-born striker Brian Clark in exchange for the Huddersfield midfielder and £2,500. But the newcomer's impact offered a swift answer to critics of the deal as John, who had made his name and earned an FA Cup winner's medal with Nottingham Forest, brought extra dimensions of class, steel and guile to the jaded Ashton Gate line-up.

After illness had delayed his debut by three weeks John shared in a sorry defeat at Northampton; but he then quickly settled to become a major force, twice helping the Robins to avoid relegation. An inveterate on-the-field talker and tenacious harasser of opponents, the darting link-man was always available to receive the ball, invariably the player who would bail a team-mate out of trouble. John drove the side, his bandy legs taking him to every corner of the pitch, now setting up an attack with a shrewd pass, then breaking up a raid with a timely tackle.

A spirited individual, he clashed with Tottenham's Dave Mackay – not an activity to be undertaken lightly – during an FA Cup tie at White Hart Lane in March 1967. Not surprisingly he got the worst of it, and the referee appeared to be on the point of dismissing Dave when John successfully interceded on his countryman's behalf, a chivalrous and honest act that typified his attitude.

When another Scot, Gordon Low, was dropped after the sacking of Fred Ford in September 1967, John was the obvious choice as captain. He proved a natural in the role, earning the respect of colleagues and exerting a beneficial influence on the club's youngsters. When new boss Alan Dicks opted to replace him with the more youthful Bobby Kellard at the end of that season, John departed for three years' stout service with Mansfield before retirement. For Bristol City he had proved a short-term investment, but a canny one.

GLYN RILEY

FLAMBOYANT YORKSHIREMAN Glyn Riley brought a whiff of optimism and, perhaps even more importantly, a dash of colour to Ashton Gate just when it was most needed. His bouncy, battling presence in the City attack, that characteristic mane of black curls flowing behind him, was like a beacon of light for the long-suffering fans.

He arrived on a free transfer from Barnsley in the summer of 1982 to find the Robins' fortunes at a depressingly low ebb. Having survived an uncomfortably close brush with oblivion during a grave financial crisis earlier in the year, City had been relegated to the Fourth Division for the first time in their history. Dark days indeed, but Glyn had no truck with prophets of doom.

The indomitable striker had headed south to revive his own flagging career, and went about it in a positive manner, his breezy confidence and professional attitude doing much to encourage his callow colleagues in Terry Cooper's inexperienced team. On the field Glyn could be an inspiration, the type of direct, all-action opponent who doesn't allow defenders a moment's peace. When the other side had the ball he could tackle with the bite of a full-back;

when he gained possession he had the strength and skill to hold it in the face of fierce challenge until team-mates arrived to support him, a godsend to the likes of Howard Pritchard and Steve Neville in subsequent seasons.

Glyn, who could also play in midfield, topped the scoring charts in his first two seasons at Ashton Gate, his productivity initially playing a major role in steadying the ship and then helping to secure promotion. During that successful 1983/84 campaign a Riley strike often came at crucial moments, but it was two years later at Wembley that his reputation as a man for the big occasion was finally and joyfully confirmed, with two goals – a sharp drive and a header – in the Freight Rover Trophy victory over Bolton.

At such moments of triumph his unbridled exuberance became a trademark beloved of the supporters, though not always of the authorities; he once earned an FA rebuke for leaping on to the Ashton Gate fence to salute the crowd. But there was no harm in Glyn, and when he moved to Aldershot – where he spent two years before going into business in 1989 – he left as one of the most popular Robins of the decade.

BORN: Barnsley, Yorkshire, 24.7.58

CITY RECORD:

League: 184 (15) games, 61 goals

FA Cup: 13 games, 4 goals

League Cup: 14 games, 4 goals

Others: 20 (1) games, 8 goals

Total: 231 (16) games, 77 goals

CITY HONOURS:

Promotion from Fourth Division 83/4

Freight Rover Trophy 85/6

Freight Rover Trophy Finalist 86/7

OTHER CLUBS:

Barnsley 74/5-81/2 (130, 16)

Doncaster Rovers on loan 79/80 (8, 2)

Torquay United on loan 87/8 (6, 1)

Aldershot 87/8-88/9 (58, 5)

TOM RITCHIE

1972/73 — 1980/81 & 1982/83 — 1984/85

WHEN TOM RITCHIE ARRIVED at Ashton Gate, he was advised to keep well clear of the plughole in the team bath. He was a pipe-cleaner on legs, the spindliest of teenagers who looked as though the first firm tackle would snap him in two. Yet the likeable Scot was destined to serve the Robins with skill and dedication in all four divisions, emerging as a credit to himself, Bristol City and the game of football.

Ironically it was his younger brother Steve, a schoolboy star at full-back, who made the biggest initial impact at the club. There were those who thought Steve had a big future, while Ritchie Snr would make an early exit after helping his talented sibling to settle in. In fact Steve played one first-team game before leaving for an unremarkable career elsewhere, and Tom was an Ashton Gate fixture – an 18-month interlude with Sunderland aside – for a decade and a half.

One thing was clear from his first training session; if work-rate was any criterion, then Tom would make the grade. He rapidly became one of manager Alan Dicks's fittest players, and after making a fine Second Division debut against Millwall in August 1972, he soon claimed a regular place on the right side of midfield. Although short of pace, Tom boasted neat control, smooth passing ability and apparently limitless stamina which enabled him to make penetrating runs from deep positions.

Despite such success Dicks detected new potential, and in 1975/76 he moved Ritchie forward to become Paul Cheesley's striking partner, with gratifying results. The Scot finished the term as leading scorer with 18 goals – in the process attracting overtures from Arsenal, which were rebuffed – and the Robins went up. In the top flight, where he sometimes reverted to his former role, Tom was not as prolific. But he earned a reputation as an awkward customer, an aerial threat who often stole in for blind-side strikes, though he was never the most clinical of finishers.

In 1981, with the club back in the Second, Tom accepted a £180,000 move to Roker Park, thus missing the trauma of the Ashton Gate Eight financial crisis. But the north-east didn't suit him and he returned to help City climb out of the Fourth, into which they had nose-dived in his absence. His experience was a key factor and, at 32, he still had much to offer when he made a surprisingly early League exit to join Yeovil Town in 1984. But no matter; by then Tom, a modest, humorous man who became a postman, had already ensured his place in the Robins' hall of fame.

BORN: Edinburgh, 2.1.52

CITY RECORD:

League: 400 (14) games, 102 goals

FA Cup: 24 (2) games, 7 goals

League Cup: 27 (1) games, 4 goals

Others: 35 games, 19 goals

Total: 486 (17) games, 132 goals

CITY HONOURS:

Promotion from Second Division 75/6

Promotion from Fourth Division 83/4

Anglo-Scottish Cup 77/8

OTHER CLUBS:

Sunderland 80/1-81/2 (35, 8)

Carlisle United on loan 81/2 (15, 0)

DENNIS ROBERTS

1938/39 — 1953/54

FOOLHARDY WAS THE FORWARD who dwelt on the ball in the vicinity of warrior centre-half Dennis Roberts, the brawny bulwark of the Bristol City rearguard who made his debut before the war and continued as the Robins' defensive mainstay until the mid-1950s. Beloved of the Ashton Gate fans for his blood-and-thunder approach, Dennis often seemed to be battling the opposition on his own, roaming freely and dispensing the most ferocious challenges en route, like some footloose buccaneer.

He was an enthusiastic devotee of the sliding tackle, which as performed by the charging stopper often used to deposit ball and man over the touchline. Though his natural impetuosity sometimes pulled him out of position, his speed at recovery was astonishing for a six-footer, and often he reappeared in the goal-mouth in the nick of time to make a desperate intervention.

Dennis was masterful in the air – he excelled in several encounters with the great Tommy Lawton – and usually he was thrown into attack for the last ten minutes of a game if the Robins were trailing. He was prone to struggle, however, if confronted by a skilful, more elusive opponent who was not interested in a toe-to-toe physical contest.

Although such an encounter with Dennis was almost inevitably a bruising affair, he was not a malicious man, which was just as well in the light of one titanic collision with the equally formidable Gordon Brice of Reading in the early 1950s. The two soccer stormtroopers made simultaneous contact with the ball, and City eye-witnesses swore that the leather changed shape from round to oval. Had there been ill intent on either side, they reckoned, then bones would have been scattered all over the pitch.

In fact, when Dennis was on the receiving end, he was always ready to take his punishment without moaning, and once made colleagues blanch by calmly pouring iodine into a hideous six-inch gash on his shin before pushing the broken skin back into place and carrying on as though nothing had happened.

The indomitable pivot, who had been rejected by Notts County as a youngster, continued as a Robins regular until a serious injury sidelined him for several months in 1952/53, and Jack White was signed. Thereafter the two played in harness for half a season until Dennis retired to run a Bristol pub. For a man whose career had been stunted by the war, he had made a mighty mark on Ashton Gate history.

BORN: Bretton, Nottinghamshire, 5.2.18

DIED: Huddersfield, Yorkshire, 8.4.01

CITY RECORD:

League: 306 games, 2 goals

FA Cup: 25 games, 0 goals

Others: 2 games, 0 goals

Total: 333 games, 2 goals

ARNOLD RODGERS

1949/50 — 1955/56

ARNOLD RODGERS was never the most elegant of centre-forwards, but how well he knew his business. Not for him the extravagant flourish or the crowd-pleasing trick; he was intent merely on finding the net by the most direct and efficient route, and he did so with a ruthless regularity which, had he been born a quarter of a century later, might have made him his fortune.

Perhaps the greatest tribute to the Rodgers method was that he did not miss many of the easy chances so often squandered by more artistic, less practical marksmen. He was quick and strong, his early days as a miner having further developed a naturally robust build, and he carried a fierce shot in either foot. A menace in the air and an intelligent reader of the game, Arnold was also adept at turning adroitly and shielding the ball under pressure – no mean feat in the days before the tackle from behind was outlawed – and team-mates often benefited from his bravery.

The Yorkshireman's £5,000 signing from First Division Huddersfield Town in November 1949 probably ranked as City manager Bob Wright's most significant contribution to the Ashton Gate cause during his brief reign. Arnold had scored 17 times in 28 top-flight outings for the Terriers, and Bob believed that he would prove a potent spearhead in the Third Division South. And so it proved.

The newcomer scored on his debut, a 4-1 away defeat at the hands of a Tommy Lawton-inspired Notts County, and went on to strike up a productive partnership with Welsh international George Lowrie. But it was his still deadlier link with the young John Atyeo, forged in 1951/52 and destined to last for four seasons, that was to prove most profitable. Both men scored freely – in 1952/53 Arnold hit the target 26 times in 33 games – and the Robins progressed from promotion hopefuls to Champions by mid-decade. He was removed from the title run-in by an Achilles tendon injury and, by then in his thirties, he never re-established himself in the side, eventually joining Shrewsbury Town to complete his playing career.

Arnold, whose son David gave Bristol City doughty service as a centre-half in the 1970s, later became a successful non-League manager with Welton Rovers and Bath City, as well as succeeding as a Bristol florist. He showed himself to be as enterprising in business as he was in football, remaining very much his own man until his death in 1993.

BORN: Rotherham, Yorkshire, 5.12.23

DIED: Bristol, 6.10.93

CITY RECORD:

League: 195 games, 106 goals

FA Cup: 9 games, 5 goals

Total: 204 games, 111 goals

CITY HONOURS:

Third Division South Championship 54/5

OTHER CLUBS:

Huddersfield Town 46/7-49/50 (28, 17)

Shrewsbury Town 56/7 (13, 3)

DAVID RODGERS

1970/71 — 1981/82

ONLY A MAN with shoulders the width of Weston pier could have handled such a weight of expectation. Following in the mighty footsteps of his famous father Arnold – one of the greatest goal-scorers in City folklore – decreed that life at Ashton Gate was never going to be easy for the son.

After 18-year-old David netted on his debut, the trophy engravers started sharpening their tools in anticipation of another record breaker. As it turned it out, the muscular central defender was never likely to grab national acclaim, but Bristol City could never have wished for a more willing and doughty servant.

Such was his strength of character that throughout his playing days he ignored crippling pains in his knees, which would have ended the careers of lesser men. Gerry Sweeney recalled watching David grimace in the treatment room as physiotherapist Les Bardsley gave him the once-over early in his time at Ashton Gate. 'Your knees are shattered,' said Les.

But the words fell on deaf ears and the big-hearted Bristolian forced his way into contention. David was tall, and tremendous in the air, but also he was adept with the ball at his feet. Thus the modern thoughtful approach of calm build-up play from the back formed the basis of City's rise to the top echelon of English football during the late 1970s.

After Rodgers had featured prominently for England Schoolboys, Ashton Gate boss Alan Dicks was delighted to sign the burly 17-year-old, who was never afraid to put his foot in where it hurt. He had been nurtured through the ranks by City's disciplinarian coach, John Sillett. Thus David – like his team-mates Gary Collier, Ray Cashley, Kevin Mabbutt, Trevor Tainton, Geoff Merrick, Keith Fear and Chris Garland – was shaped by that hardline approach in his early days.

Despite scoring in his opening senior appearance, in a League Cup win against Leicester at Ashton Gate in November 1970, Big Dave was really in his element when he was marshalling the back line. At first he formed an awesome pairing with Merrick and was an integral part of City's 1974 FA Cup run when they starred on the front page of *The Times* for slaying mighty Leeds United. He was imperious against Liverpool in the sixth round as well, but the Merseysiders squeezed through 1-0 and eventually won the trophy.

After a spell on the fringes of the side as City clinched promotion, David regained his first-team berth at the expense of Gary Collier, who was sold to Coventry City in a record £325,000 deal in 1979.

Not once did David let the club down during more than a decade of sterling service and it was hard lines when he become one of the Ashton Gate Eight, who lost their livelihoods. Later he moved on to Torquay, Lincoln and Forest Green Rovers and in 2005 he was working at Clifton College. Even with dodgy knees, Big Dave took it all in his stride.

BORN: Bristol, 28.2.52

CITY RECORD:

League: 190 (2) games, 15 goals

FA Cup: 18 (1) games, 1 goal

League Cup: 16 games, 2 goals

Others: 12 games, 0 goals

Total: 236 (3) games,18 goals

OTHER CLUBS:

Torquay United 81/2 (5, 1)

Lincoln City 81/2 (3, 0)

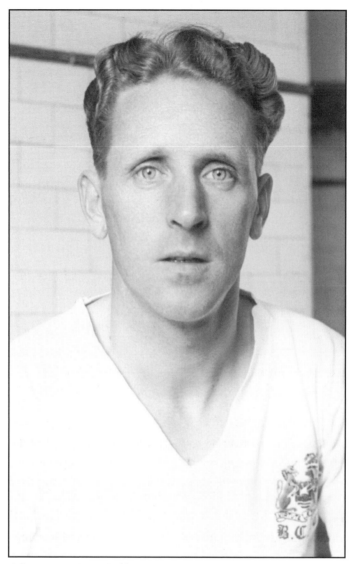

BORN: Wednesbury, Staffordshire, 31.12.29
DIED: North Somerset, 12.96

CITY RECORD:

League: 270 games, 102 goals

FA Cup: 16 games, 6 goals

League Cup: 1 game, 0 goals

Others: 1 game, 0 goals

Total: 288 games, 108 goals

CITY HONOURS:

Third Division South Championship 54/5

OTHER CLUBS:

Coventry City 56/7-58/9 (76, 27)

JIMMY ROGERS

1950/51 — 1956/57 & 1958/59 — 1961/62

JIMMY ROGERS was a livewire opportunist who delighted in telling the world that he was lethal in front of goal – from six inches! What modesty precluded him from adding was that, for two seasons in the mid-1950s, when he scored 50 times in 78 League games, he was one of the most prolific and versatile forwards outside the top flight.

The fair-haired Midlander, equally effective on the wing or leading the attack, was a fast and gritty raider who would have merited the nickname of 'Sniffer' long before it was coined for the England striker Allan Clarke. Jimmy had an instinct for rebounds that verged on the uncanny. If a shot by John Atyeo or Arnold Rodgers was too hard for the goalkeeper to hold, then the odds were that the nimble little poacher would be on hand to slip it over the line.

Jimmy, who joined Bristol City on a free transfer from Wolves in May 1950 after white-hot Molineux competition had prevented a First Division breakthrough, boasted fine ball control, but he owed much of his success to determination. He was firmly of the 'if-they-kick-me-then-I'll-kick-them-back' persuasion, and hulking defenders soon got the message that they were not going to intimidate Jimmy Rogers.

For four seasons he battled to establish a regular place, playing in every forward position and making useful contributions in each. But it was during 1954/55 that he made his biggest impact to date. After he had enjoyed an impressive five-month spell at outside-right, he was switched to centre-forward because of injury to Arnold Rodgers and responded with a rush of goals, 15 in 18 outings, to finish with a tally of 25 and help clinch the Third Division South title.

There were those who thought such marksmanship was a flash in the pan, but Jimmy proved them wrong in City's first post-war season in Division Two, again wearing the number-nine shirt and again netting 25 times. In view of his strike-rate, his move down a flight to Coventry City, along with team-mate Jack Boxley in 1956, surprised many. But new Ashton Gate boss Peter Doherty soon brought him back to Bristol for £3,500 and he flourished once more, being one of the few who found form during the 1959/60 relegation season.

On retirement from League football in 1962, Jimmy, a humorous and intelligent man, enjoyed success as player-manager of Cinderford Town before becoming one of the team that ran a wildlife park at Westbury-on-Trym.

BORN: Liverpool, 8.4.49

CITY RECORD:

League: 100 (1) games, 18 goals

FA Cup: 4 games, 0 goals

League Cup: 6 (1) games, 2 goals

Others: 6 (2) games, 1 goal

Total: 116 (4) games, 21 goals

OTHER CLUBS:

Everton 65/6-74/5 (232, 102)

Manchester City 74/5-77/8 (99, 23)

Norwich City 80/1-81/2 (42, 9)

6 England caps (2 won with Everton, 4 with Manchester City) 1971-77

MANAGER:

Oldham Athletic 1982-94

Everton 1994-97

Manchester City 1998-2001

Ipswich Town 2002-

JOE ROYLE

IT WAS THE MOST ELOQUENT of introductions. Joe Royle, on loan from Manchester City but with a view to a permanent move, scored four times from only four chances on his Robins debut, and manager Alan Dicks was soon dusting off the welcome mat. City fans were ecstatic, and understandably so. They had not hailed a traditional goal-scoring hero since injury had put an untimely end to Paul Cheesley's career; and, in that crushing victory over Middlesbrough in the autumn of 1977, Joe had given Ashton Gate a performance to savour.

A £90,000 deal was completed in an atmosphere of heady expectation, but a return to earth was imminent. In the wake of his spectacular entrance, the England centre-forward – he had played for his country only six months earlier – experienced an 11-match goal famine, the first of several such periods of poverty during his City sojourn.

But Joe, to whom Dicks had turned after an approach for Newcastle's Alan Gowling had failed, had too much class and experience to become rattled, and his all-round competence as target man, providing chances rather than taking them, fully justified his place in the side. His ability to shield the ball under pressure – team-mates could pass to Joe with confidence that possession would not be squandered – was an integral part of the Robins' tactics, and the goal tallies of Kevin Mabbutt and Tom Ritchie were boosted significantly by the big man's subtle contribution.

The respect and warmth in which the genial Merseysider was held by his colleagues was never more obvious than in November 1978, when he ended one of his lengthier barren sequences with a double strike against Bolton. Their spontaneous explosion of pleasure and relief that his ordeal was over far exceeded any routine celebration of a goal.

When City were relegated in 1979/80 Joe moved on to Norwich, giving the Canaries two years' splendid service before seeking a job in management. One of his first applications was to Ashton Gate, in respect of the seat left vacant by the 1982 sacking of Roy Hodgson, but he was pipped by Terry Cooper. Instead, he took over at Oldham, building a name as one of soccer's more level-headed bosses, earning national celebrity with the Latics' heroic knockout campaigns of 1990, then winning the FA Cup with Everton in 1995. When the tabloids twigged his engaging personality, they dubbed him 'Mr Nice Guy' and 'Gentleman Joe'; his old friends in Bristol were not a bit surprised.

MARTIN SCOTT

1990/91 — 1994/95

THIS PRIZE-FIGHTER FLOATED like a butterfly and stung like a bee. Martin Scott was always destined to punch among the heavyweights. Off the pitch he stayed tight-lipped, keeping his guard high. However, inside his 'ring' he was a real terrier of a left-back, just as menacing in the tackle as he was during countless bursts forward. Everything about his game was characterised by gusto and enthusiasm, and in his four years at Ashton Gate, Martin Scott was one of the most popular members of the Bristol City squad.

Versatility, pace and tenacity were the Yorkshireman's exceptional strengths and, despite his small stature, there were few tasks on a football field that he did not carry out with the utmost competence.

Even in his rookie days, managers knew they would get everything from the dedicated Martin. As a teenager, he made his League debut for Rotherham before he had even signed professional terms. He was the Merry Millers' most impressive performer during the late 1980s and his dogged displays in midfield helped them to clinch the Fourth Division title.

City had been keeping tabs on Scott's progress for several years before a bid was accepted, and he became one of Jimmy Lumsden's first signings following the departure of Joe Jordan in 1990. The £200,000 fee was the biggest Rotherham had ever received, but the newly-promoted Robins were confident they had recruited a player with the ability to match their lofty ambitions.

Martin thrived after taking the step up, enjoying his finest campaign in 1991/92, when his endless endeavour down the left flank was a colossal factor in ensuring that City beat the drop into the Third Division. Despite managerial upheavals at the club, Martin was ever-present and deservedly won the player of the year award. With his reputation soaring and top-flight clubs making their interest known, the dynamic little full-back began to gain a taste for goals. He became chief free-kick and penalty taker, contributing key strikes as City continued to upset the bookies and avoid relegation in following years.

Eventually the Robins caved in to the big money, valuing Martin at £750,000 in the exchange deal which brought midfielder Gary Owers from Sunderland in December 1994. Many fans felt it was no coincidence that just a few months later, City's five-year stay in the second tier ended.

Martin was a key part of Sunderland's 1996 First Division title success under Peter Reid. Initially he impressed in the Premiership, too, but an unfortunate succession of injuries and the emergence of young Michael Gray curtailed his progress.

Later Martin excelled in an extremely successful coaching set-up with Neale Cooper at Hartlepool. Despite their shoestring budget, United became one of City's main rivals for promotion over several seasons and, as ever, the former Ashton Gate favourite revelled in the cut and thrust of competition. That surprised no one who knew one of life's born winners.

BORN: Sheffield, 7.1.68

CITY RECORD:

League: 171 games, 14 goals

FA Cup: 10 games, 0 goals

League Cup: 11 games, 1 goal

Others: 8 games, 1 goal

Total: 200 games, 16 goals

OTHER CLUBS:

Rotherham United 84/5-90/1 (94, 3)

Sunderland 94/5-98/9 (106, 9)

BORN: Gloucester, 17.3.46

CITY RECORD:

League: 149 (4) games, 48 goals

FA Cup: 7 games, 2 goals

League Cup: 18 games, 4 goals

Total: 174 (4) games, 54 goals

GERRY SHARPE

1964/65 — 1970/71

THERE WAS A SICKENING CRACK that could be heard all around Ashton Gate. The crowd grew hushed as trainer Les Bardsley sprinted on to the field, fearing the worst and finding it. Gerry Sharpe's leg had been shattered in a tackle with Eric McMordie of Middlesbrough, and the wound was so hideous that players on both sides turned away in anguish. City's slim winger cum inside-forward was never to play again.

That harrowing incident in January 1971 deprived the Robins of one of their brightest prospects in years. Gerry, then two months short of his 25th birthday, had recently been in scintillating form and was surely destined for greater glory, perhaps at Ashton Gate, or more likely with one of the top clubs already monitoring his progress.

It was easy to understand the giants' interest. Lining up alongside a big central striker, as he did in his early days under Fred Ford, Gerry could be a lethal force. In crowded penalty areas he was the nimblest of poachers, nipping artfully in front of defenders to capitalise on the slightest mistake. Effective in the air for a small man, he packed a fierce shot in both feet and was a cool finisher, as he proved in snatching six goals in an 11-match run imme-diately after making his debut as an 18-year-old in autumn 1964.

But probably he was seen to best advantage on the left flank, where he was usually played by Fred's managerial successor, Alan Dicks. The number-11 slot gave him extra space to use his speed, and when Gerry took players on he was a joy to watch. He scored many of his most spectacular goals when cutting into the box after beating a full-back, and he had an instinct for pouncing on rebounds.

Willingness to fight for the ball when the opposition gained possession was another Sharpe speciality, particularly in his wing role. He would toil tirelessly up and down his touchline, harassing opponents in the manner of Arsenal's George Armstrong, an attribute that would have served him well in the worka-holics' paradise of the modern game.

After his enforced retirement Gerry became City's youth team coach, and in 1982 he enjoyed a 19-day spell as caretaker-manager, during which the Robins lost only one out of six games, following the sacking of Roy Hodgson. Later he went to live and work in the United States, no doubt reflecting on what might have been but for that fateful challenge that cut him down on the verge of his prime.

BORN: Stirling, 4.2.54

CITY RECORD:

League: 295 games, 0 goals

FA Cup: 16 games, 0 goals

League Cup: 19 games, 0 goals

Others: 27 games, 0 goals

Total: 357 games, 0 goals

CITY HONOURS:

Promotion from Fourth Division 83/4

Anglo-Scottish Cup 77/8

OTHER CLUBS:

Exeter City 85/6-87/8 (109, 0)

JOHN SHAW

WHEN SCOTTISH GOALKEEPER John Shaw left Elland Road in the summer of 1974 after three steady seasons as a Leeds United reserve, he had little notion of the rollercoaster ride that awaited him at Ashton Gate. During the 11 years that followed he was to experience a bewildering succession of highs and lows which would have driven a less resilient character to despair. There were heady spells as a First Division regular, several axings and corresponding comebacks, a distressing illness which deprived him of his hair, and a frustrating interlude on the fringe of an international breakthrough that never came.

Yet John's days as a Robin had a deceptively mundane beginning. After heading south on a free transfer, together with midfielder Jimmy Mann, he was destined for two seasons in second- and third-team football before a loss of form by Ray Cashley offered the first hint of an opportunity at the top level. Even then it was Len Bond who got the first call, but the fates had not forgotten John. Poor Len was injured after two games and in October 1976 the patient Scot stepped into the breach, there to remain for more than a century of consecutive matches.

It was during this exalted period that he was spoken of as a possible alternative to the much maligned Alan Rough between his country's posts. Though the summons didn't come, John continued in splendid form, handling crosses with confidence, showing agility on his line and vociferously organising his defence. A slight weakness in his kicking had been eradicated, and he seemed in no imminent danger of replacement. But in February 1980, with the Robins sliding towards Division Two, a few mistakes crept in, and Cashley was recalled.

After a brief return to first-team duty, there followed a difficult time for the former Leeds man. Swedish 'keeper Jan Moller was recruited and John's alopecia, a condition which causes baldness, was worsening. But Jan departed in the wake of City's 1982 cash crisis, and the old cry of 'Send for Shaw' went up once again. He came into a side on the way down to the Fourth Division, soon recaptured his best form, and played a leading role in earning promotion two years later before joining Exeter in 1985. John's unquenchable spirit in the face of adversity won widespread admiration, and he could always joke with team-mates about his shining pate. As he told them: 'You try playing behind the City defence for 11 years and see what you look like!'

ALAN SKIRTON

1968/69 — 1970/71

WHEN ALAN SKIRTON was offered the chance to return to his native West Country in November 1968, the big, bold, goal-scoring winger was only two months short of his 30th birthday. But he could still fly a bit, and the challenge of helping to rescue Bristol City from their plight near the foot of the Second Division was especially appealing to a man who had been rejected by the Robins as a teenage amateur. Accordingly, a £15,000 deal was struck with Blackpool and the former Arsenal star played a stirring part in the Ashton Gate club's successful bid to beat the drop for a third consecutive season.

Alan's game was simple, but there weren't many who relished facing him. He liked to receive the ball in space and run at defenders, aiming to steam past them on the outside and cross the ball at speed, or cut inside for a crack at goal. Standing just an inch short of six feet and blessed with the powerful build of a traditional British centre-forward, he was a fearsome sight for all but the most stout-hearted of opponents.

The West Country crowd took to the experienced flankman at once – after all, he was one of their own – and his arrival was also welcomed by striker John Galley, who thrived on his service. As for Alan, he enjoyed the home games, when City would be committed to attack, but was less than captivated by manager Alan Dicks' 4-4-2 away formation, which meant he was deployed in an alien role as midfield hustler.

Not surprisingly in these circumstances, Ashton Gate was the setting for the majority of Alan's finest performances, and all but one of his 14 League goals for the Robins. Also it was the scene of a devastating personal display in a League Cup encounter with Rotherham in September 1970. The draw for the next round meant that if City progressed they would face his former club, Blackpool. He was more than keen to renew acquaintance with the Seasiders and worked tirelessly to inspire a 4-0 win, scoring once and showing his most convincing form of the season.

The amiable Bathonian's next goal in the competition was more crucial, being struck past Pat Jennings in the drawn first leg of the semi-final against Spurs. The second leg was lost, so there was no trip to Wembley, and at the end of that season Alan, by now 32, accepted a free transfer to Torquay. He went on to become a successful commercial manager, first with Bath City and then Yeovil Town, to complete the happiest of homecomings.

BORN: Bath, Somerset, 23.1.39

CITY RECORD:

League: 75 (3) games, 14 goals

FA Cup: 2 games, 2 goals

League Cup: 13 games, 2 goals

Total: 90 (3) games, 18 goals

OTHER CLUBS:

Arsenal 60/1-66/7 (144, 53)

Blackpool 66/7-68/9 (77, 26)

Torquay United 71/2 (38, 7)

BORN: Glasgow, 10.7.45

CITY RECORD:

League: 396 (10) games, 22 goals

FA Cup: 23 games, 1 goal

League Cup: 27 games, 4 goals

Others: 33 games, 2 goals

Total: 479 (10) games, 29 goals

CITY HONOURS:

Promotion from Second Division 75/6

Anglo-Scottish Cup 77/8

OTHER CLUBS:

Morton 66/7-70/1 (139, 16)

York City 81/2 (12, 0)

GERRY SWEENEY

1971/72 — 1981/82

GERRY SWEENEY was a reliable sort of chap, an eminently efficient right-back who did his job, week-in and week-out, with the minimum of fuss. The fans appreciated his presence, but perhaps took him for granted, hardly seeing the enthusiastic Glaswegian as a potential match-winner. Yet Gerry's all-round talents were sorely under-estimated, and he proved it in the promotion spring of 1976.

By March the Robins' hopes of climbing into the First Division were high, but injuries forced manager Alan Dicks into changes, and Gerry was pushed forward into midfield. He responded with a succession of stirring performances, displaying both vision and apparently limitless stamina, and at one stage he scored three goals in four games to keep the City bandwagon rolling. His winner against West Bromwich Albion, fellow contenders for a place in the top flight, was particularly welcome, but for the connoisseur there was nothing to match the crisp volley with which he rounded off a sweet seven-man move to secure a point against Sunderland, the eventual champions, at Roker Park.

In fact Gerry, who reclaimed the number-two shirt when the squad returned to full strength, should have surprised no one with his expertise. When he arrived in Bristol in August 1971 – as a £22,000 signing from Morton, who had rebuilt his career after being freed by Celtic – most of his experience had been on the wing. His first Robins campaign was spent in midfield, but Alan Dicks cannily converted him into a right-back, a role in which his composure, control and ability to read the game made him a prime asset for a decade.

Gerry's contribution was as effective in the First Division as in the Third, and it's a tribute to his phenomenal fitness – his team-mates nicknamed him 'Yifter the Shifter', after the great African athlete, because he always won the cross-country races in training – that he played League football until he was nearly 37. He left the club as one of the Ashton Gate Eight during the financial upheaval of 1982, and after a brief stint at York City and a spell as Walsall's assistant manager, he became a postman in the Bristol area. He continued to grace a high level of amateur soccer as he reached his mid-forties, later returning to the Robins as a coach and relishing a period as Joe Jordan's number-two.

An ebullient dressing-room jester renowned for his mimicry, Gerry was deadly serious when he took the field, and will go down as a major influence on the most successful City side for nearly 70 years.

BORN: Bristol, 8.6.48

CITY RECORD:

League: 456 (30) games, 24 goals

FA Cup: 31 games, 3 goals

League Cup: 35 (3) games, 0 goals

Others: 34 games, 3 goals

Total: 556 (33) games, 30 goals

CITY HONOURS:

Promotion from Second Division 75/6

Anglo-Scottish Cup 77/8

OTHER CLUBS:

Torquay United 81/2 (19, 1)

TREVOR TAINTON

1967/68 — 1981/82

WHEN BRISTOL CITY were promoted to the First Division in 1976, there were pundits who predicted the worst for midfield workhorse Trevor Tainton. They reckoned he simply didn't have enough class to rub shoulders with the best in the land, and that his unobtrusive style would be largely ineffective in the top flight. If such pessimists had reflected a little more deeply before delivering their verdict, they might have recalled that in the early 1970s a certain Bill Shankly had thought highly enough of Trevor's potential to offer £50,000 for his services. The astute Liverpool boss wasn't often wrong in his assessment of a footballer, and so it proved in the case of the stocky Bristolian.

While not exactly causing a sensation among the elite – charisma was never his strong suit – Tainton more than held his own. His tackling and work-rate were all that might have been expected, but as his confidence grew there was also a marked improvement in his distribution and positional play. Trevor would receive the ball wide on the right and pass it on briskly, rarely losing possession, and when the opposition threatened he was an adept interceptor of passes. Perhaps the most disappointing aspect of his game was a humble scoring record of one goal in every 18 starts, an abject tally for a man with a strong shot.

Trevor had made his City debut nine years earlier in one of the last games before Fred Ford was sacked as manager. New boss Alan Dicks gave him plenty of opportunities, but he failed to establish himself fully until he was converted into an orthodox outside-right following the departure of Alan Skirton in 1971. For a time the versatile Trevor, who was also a capable deputy right-back, impressed in his new role. But after a sequence of indifferent displays he reverted to midfield, where he settled to become an integral part of the side.

Having risen with the Robins from near the foot of the Second Division to the exalted reaches of the First, and then slid with them back down to the Third, Trevor had well and truly paid his dues. Over 14 campaigns he had played nearly 600 games – a total exceeded only by John Atyeo – and deserved a more fitting farewell than his sad exit as one of the Ashton Gate Eight during the 1982 financial crisis.

Trevor Tainton was a quiet, neat man who enjoyed a quiet, neat career. But for all that, it was a valuable one, and Bristol City would have been the poorer without it.

BOB TAYLOR

1988/89 — 1991/92

THE ASHTON GATE FAITHFUL had expected a useful player when Joe Jordan handed over £225,000 for a Leeds United reserve in the spring of 1989, but Bob Taylor was a gem beyond their dreams. Joe had acquired a man obsessed, in the nicest possible way, of course. Scoring goals was Bob's passion, and in 1989/90 he indulged it freely and often sensationally as the Robins climbed – rather creakily in the end, as he was absent with a springtime injury – into the Second Division. Where lesser men might have dithered, the dashing north-easterner shot on sight to become the first City marksman to find the net 30 times in a season since the heyday of John Atyeo.

Such a feat was prodigious in itself, but it was the quality of his strikes as much as their abundance that awed his audience. Bob would habitually lash the ball home from outside the box – often on the volley, as when completing his hat-trick with a booming dipper against Crewe at Ashton Gate in April 1990 – and some of his aerial work was inspired. He was adept at quicksilver turns in tight spaces and was always capable of the unexpected, such as the overhead kick that stunned Birmingham in the first home match of the promotion season. And it wasn't as though Bob did nothing but score. He excelled in passing movements, linking his line in the old-fashioned way and showing a deft touch on the ball. No wonder irreverent team-mates nicknamed him God; they reckoned he could perform the impossible.

There was, however, one minor drawback to the unassuming newcomer's insatiable appetite for goals; when he experienced a brief spell of missing the target, as all strikers must, it affected his whole game. Suddenly his powers of control and distribution deserted him, and he looked out of place on a football field. Happily, when that next shot found the net, he was transformed, revelling in every facet of his work, and he was so thrilled to be presented with the match ball following one hat-trick that he kept it beside him all evening.

Such souvenirs proved harder to come by in Division Two, but Bob continued to carry a major threat at the higher level and most supporters were devastated when the prolific 24-year-old stepped back into the Third to join West Bromwich Albion for £300,000 in January 1992.

Predictably he scored freely at the Hawthorns, where his strike-rate earned him cult status and he helped to earn promotion in 1993/94. There followed Premiership experience with Bolton and in a second stint for the Baggies, and the evergreen predator was still banging in the goals for Cheltenham Town in 2004 at the age of 37.

BORN: Easington, County Durham, 3.2.67

CITY RECORD

League: 96 (10) games, 50 goals

FA Cup: 9 (1) games, 5 goals

League Cup: 6 (1) games, 2 goals

Others: 3 games, 1 goal

Total: 114 (12) games, 58 goals

CITY HONOURS:

Promotion from Third Division 89/90

OTHER CLUBS:

Leeds United 85/6-88/9 (42, 9)

West Bromwich Albion 91/2-97/8 (238, 96)

Bolton Wanderers initially on loan 97/8-99/00 (77, 21)

West Bromwich Albion 99/00-02/03 (86, 17)

Cheltenham Town 03/04 (28, 7)

SHAUN TAYLOR

1996/97 — 1999/2000

SHAUN TAYLOR'S IMPACT on Bristol City's back line was colossal. The West Country warhorse was the bravest, most uncompromising leader at Ashton Gate since Norman Hunter hung up his size-10 clobbers. Like old 'Bite Yer Legs', Shaun arrived in the twilight of his playing career but went on to become one of the club's most influential defenders during gleeful days in south Bristol. Eventually, the Devon giant's overall contribution to the Robins cause stretched to nearly nine years, including an influential coaching stint.

At the grand old age of 33, Taylor checked in at the club as a man scorned. Having been a talisman for Swindon Town as the Wiltshiremen enjoyed one of the most successful periods in their history, the big fella was judged surplus to requirements by County Ground boss Steve McMahon, who believed that his captain's best days were behind him. Thus, when Joe Jordan enquired about his availability in 1996, Shaun packed his bags to head down the M4 the following day.

To the surprise of some observers, the glowering man-mountain was welcomed instantly by the often sceptical Gate faithful, even after switching local allegiances. While his touch and distribution were basic, Taylor's battling qualities overwhelmed his technical flaws and John Ward shrewdly built his team around him after Jordan's exit.

He combined brilliantly with the more elegant Louis Carey at centre-back and often was among the goals as City recovered from a trough to claim a play-off spot in 1997, then sealed promotion to Division One in the following season.

In a modern game so bereft of on-field charisma, Shaun was a true blast from the old school. He relished the hot-tempered derbies with Rovers and never lost to the blue-and-white quarters throughout his time at the club. Typically, after suffering one hideously gory head injury against the Pirates, he refused to leave the field, and played on for several weeks with heavy bandaging.

Shaun had been a massive presence throughout the 1997/98 promotion campaign, but his season ended abruptly and agonisingly. During City's crucial showdown with Graham Taylor's Watford, the eventual Champions, Shaun ruptured a cruciate ligament. As he was 35, the widespread belief was that the big defender would call it a day, but that merely fuelled his determination to return.

Accordingly ten months later, after surgery, he was back in the fray, though he proved unable to rescue a crisis-torn side which was floundering distressingly under the guidance of Benny Lennartsson, and the club made a swift return to Division Two.

Begrudgingly Shaun retired in 2000 due to persistent fitness niggles, but he aspired to a future in management and accepted a role as reserve team coach at Ashton Gate, helping to nurture defenders Matt Hill and Danny Coles on their way to the senior side. He left the club in the summer of 2005.

BORN: Plymouth, 26.2.63

CITY RECORD:

League: 105 games, 7 goals

FA Cup: 8 games, 1 goal

League Cup: 8 games, 2 goals

Others: 5 games, 0 goals

Total: 126 games, 10 goals

CITY HONOURS:

Promotion from Second Division 97/8

OTHER CLUBS:

Exeter City 86/7-90/1 (200, 17)

Swindon Town 91/2-96/7 (212, 30)

MIKE THRESHER

1954/55 — 1964/65

TO MOST RIGHT-WINGERS, a visit to Ashton Gate in the late 1950s and early 1960s was the equivalent of an afternoon in the dentist's chair (that's the traditional type, rather than the lurid version employed by Gazza and company in a Hong Kong bar). The fearful flankmen knew the experience was going to be unpleasant, but there was nothing they could do to avoid it. The reason for their trepidation? Mike Thresher, one of the fastest, hardest and most aggressive left-backs in the land.

The attackers' insuperable problem was that they just couldn't escape. If they adopted the subtle approach, all clever tricks, then Mike would tackle them like a bulldozer; if they tried to outstrip him with speed then he would tackle them like a runaway bulldozer. And, to a man, they found all that attention less flattering than flattening.

Yet the marvellous thing about Mike was that he wasn't a malicious player. Okay, he suffered a few bookings in his time – what defender doesn't? – but he was never sent off, and never set out to injure an opponent. Part of the reason for his formidable reputation was the speed at which he worked; Mike was an expert at the sliding tackle, so that any collision was likely to be a spectacular affair. There was also his apparent unconcern for the men he left on the ground. Often he took fearsome knocks himself, but it was a point of honour with the dark, curly-haired Devonian to trot away blithely from the scene of the crash, his face devoid of any expression, least of all compassion.

Mike, a winger himself in his early non-League days, first staked his claim to become Jack Bailey's long-term successor in the Robins' number-three shirt on Boxing Day 1954. He performed so ably in a victory at Reading that he remained in the side that took the Third Division South title that term, and became a fixture for the next ten years.

His most famous game was in the FA Cup, a 1959 home clash with Blackpool, in which he subdued Stanley Matthews and helped to ensure a replay at Bloomfield Road. But many who knew Mike best will remember him for his supreme enthusiasm, exemplified by his reaction to a ban for accumulated cautions in 1964. The terms of the suspension forbade him admission to Ashton Gate, yet he contrived to watch the action from the lofty vantage point of trainer Lemmo Southway's nearby flat.

Mike, who worked as a carpenter after leaving the game, might have reached the top flight had he been blessed with passing skills to match his tackling. First Division forwards, whose exposure to the Thresher menace was limited to chance cup encounters, were more than happy with the status quo.

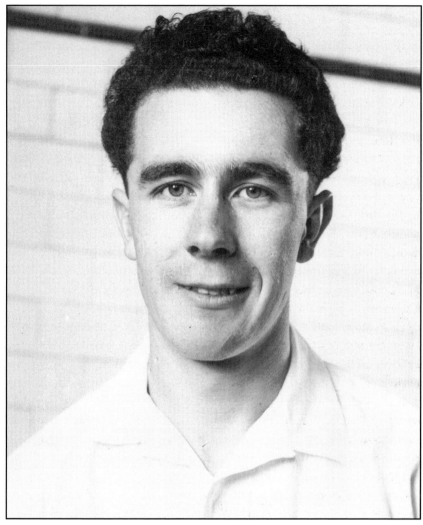

BORN: Cullompton, Devon, 9.3.31

DIED: Bristol, 28.12.99

CITY HONOURS:

Third Division South Championship 54/5

CITY RECORD:

League: 379 games, 1 goal

FA Cup: 29 games, 0 goals

League Cup: 6 games, 0 goals

Others: 1 game, 0 goals

Total: 415 games, 1 goal

BRIAN TINNION

1992/93 — 2004/05

THE TALE OF BRIAN TINNION and Paul Gascoigne bears more than a passing resemblance to the Tortoise and the Hare. At the starting blocks there was little to divide the two gifted Geordies during their days as teenage room-mates at Newcastle United. They both played with breathtaking vision and unerring accuracy and both were tipped to reach the top of the game.

But after leaving St James' Park, their professional paths were never to cross again. While Gascoigne dominated headlines in the early 1990s, the more sedate Tinnion signed for Bradford City. However, 15 years later, it was Brian and not close-friend Paul who could look back on a career fulfilled. Since signing for the Robins in 1993 Tinnion became a vintage Red who just got better with age. He is the finest City player of the past decade and a successful spell as manager would rank him as one of the Ashton Gate all-time greats.

Brian won over the fans within weeks of his arrival when he rattled home a decisive penalty in the dying minutes of a clash with Bristol Rovers. His graceful playing style and vision on the left captivated the crowd, sorely in need of a new hero to replace Jackie Dziekanowski.

It took Tinnion barely 12 months to enter City folklore, his brilliant effort at Anfield helping to scupper Liverpool in one of the FA Cup shocks of the decade. As a result he received national plaudits and his cultured left foot was tipped to grace the top flight. Meanwhile his upright running style and

sheer precision with crossfield passes had made him City's most identifiable player.

But, strangely, that goal marked the start of the north-easterner's most difficult period at Ashton Gate. The club slipped to Division Two and Brian found himself in exile as manager Joe Jordan returned. Suffering from glandular fever, he barely had the energy to last 90 minutes and the fickle boo-boys, who once had hailed him as a messiah, called for his head. However, he stayed, the more encouraging management style of John Ward helped bring the best from him, and he recalls City's promotion in 1998 as one of his proudest moments.

Tinnion's calm off-field persona ensured he was always a respected figure at the club's Abbots Leigh training ground, and when Danny Wilson arrived following City's return to the Second Division, the experienced midfielder would often be left to his own devices to keep himself fit. He knew exactly what was needed to ensure he would get the most from his ageing joints on match-days.

On the pitch, too, he was given more independence with a free role in central midfield. Brian enjoyed his new responsibilities and it was during this time that he decided on a future in management. He stopped sharing a room with best-mate Mickey Bell, perhaps in a move to distance himself from the boot-room banter. And in the wake of City's dismal play-off final defeat against Brighton, Tinnion was announced as the shock successor to the sacked Danny Wilson.

BORN: Stanley, County Durham, 23.2.68

CITY RECORD:

League: 418 (42) games, 36 goals

FA Cup: 28 (3) games, 6 goals

League Cup: 28 (2) games, 0 goals

Others: 23 (7) games, 0 goals

Total: 497 (54) games, 42 goals

CITY HONOURS:

Promotion from Second Division 97/8

Auto Windscreens Shield Finalist 99/00

LDV Vans Trophy 02/03

OTHER CLUBS:

Newcastle United 86/7-88/9 (32, 2)

Bradford City 88/9-92/3 (145, 22)

MANAGER:

Bristol City 2004-

BORN: Hartlepool, County Durham, 9.12.56

CITY RECORD:

League: 215 (3) games, 77 goals

FA Cup: 18 games, 3 goals

League Cup: 21 games, 8 goals

Others: 30 games, 11 goals

Total: 284 (3) games, 99 goals

CITY HONOURS:

Freight Rover Trophy 85/6

Freight Rover Trophy Finalist 86/7

OTHER CLUBS:

Middlesbrough 77/8 (3, 0)

Darlington 78/9-83/4 (251, 87)

Besiktas, Turkey, 89/90

ALAN WALSH

1984/85 — 1988/89

ALAN WALSH was the buried treasure of Ashton Gate. Hardly anyone outside the League's lower reaches had heard of him, yet he had skills that were worth a fortune . . . or, at least, considerably more than the paltry £18,000 City were ordered by a transfer tribunal to pay his former club, Darlington, in August 1984. The north-easterners had been laughed out of court for demanding £85,000 for the top scorer in their history, but after Alan's early games as a Robin it was clear that manager Terry Cooper had picked up a Rolls-Royce for a pocketful of loose change.

The creative flair and shooting power of the left-sided blond newcomer, who was especially dangerous with free-kicks, proved a devastating combination as City set about consolidating their newly-regained Third Division status. His philosophy was 'the more you shoot, the more you score' and he proceeded to pepper opponents' goals at every opportunity, from any angle and, most spectacularly, from almost any distance. But it wasn't only his howitzer-style finishing that made Alan such a glorious entertainer. Though hardly the fleetest of flankmen, he could take on opponents, befuddle them with his trickery in the tightest of spaces and lift tantalisingly curling crosses into the penalty box with that distinguished left foot.

Alan almost invariably duped defenders with the same piece of skill, but they could rarely cope with it; he would put his foot on the ball, feint to go one way and then dash past on the opposite side. One illustrious victim was West Ham full-back Ray Stewart, for whom the final whistle in a September 1984 Milk Cup encounter at Ashton Gate must have been a merciful release.

For a striker who spent so much time on the wing and in deep-lying positions, and who wasn't strong in the air for a six-footer, Alan compiled a creditable goal tally. But it is for great individual efforts, such as one rasping 20-yard drive after beating two men at Brentford, that his memory will endure.

A charming, easy-going character who sometimes attracted unfair criticism through a deceptively lazy style, Alan was a willing mixer with the fans; they held him in great affection, without perhaps fully appreciating what a gem of a player he was at City's level. It's a shame and something of a mystery that his entire English career, which ended when he accepted a lucrative move to Istanbul in 1989, was spent in relative obscurity. Alan, who later returned to Ashton Gate as a coach, possessed the talent to have graced a wider stage.

JACK WHITE
1952/53 — 1957/58

THERE WAS NEVER ANY DOUBT about who gave the orders during Bristol City's charge to the Third Division South Championship in 1954/55. Jack White, a naturally dominant personality who had known days of toil in the Yorkshire coalfields before becoming a professional footballer, was born to lead, and for five and a half seasons at Ashton Gate he did so to inspirational effect.

Manager Pat Beasley signed the steely, constructive half-back for £5,300 from Aldershot in October 1952, and immediately installed him as captain of a team that for four years had been unable to make the leap from midtable mediocrity to a position as title challengers. The Robins needed lifting and Jack, who could be devastatingly effective as an attacking wing-half but often played as defensive kingpin when the ageing Dennis Roberts was injured, set about the task with gusto.

That season City finished fifth, then came third in the next, before topping the table by nine points in mid-decade. Jack had certainly not wrought a single-handed transformation – there were many other fine players in the side – but he had been the catalyst, driving his team-mates on, and invariably offering a splendid personal example.

Though not a big man, standing 5ft 8 in, Jack was dynamic in the air, and had the knack of imparting both power and direction to headers, even when under severe pressure. He could pass accurately with either foot and was a clean striker of the ball, occasionally volleying goals from outside the penalty area, where he liked to lurk when the Robins won a corner. Such marksmanship was a throwback to his early years as a centre-forward at Aldershot, although it was also a White family trait, his younger brother Len being a successful spearhead with Newcastle United and Huddersfield Town.

Jack was 31 by the time City reached the Second Division, but his influence did not wane for several seasons. It was not until March 1958, his role of elder statesman and captain by then resting squarely with Tommy Burden, that he left Ashton Gate to become player-manager of non-League Cambridge City.

Perhaps it's because he's a northerner who, unlike many from his native county, turned his back on the West at the end of his career, but somehow Jack never attained the status and affection in City folklore his achievements deserved. It is a glaring oversight.

BORN: Doncaster, Yorkshire, 17.3.24

CITY RECORD:

League: 216 games, 11 goals

FA Cup: 11 games, 0 goals

Total: 227 games, 11 goals

CITY HONOURS:

Third Division South Championship 54/5

OTHER CLUBS:

Aldershot 46/7-52/3 (209, 24)

BORN: Birmingham, 24.11.55

CITY RECORD:

League: 209 (20) games, 10 goals

FA Cup: 8 games, 2 goals

League Cup: 16 (3) games, 2 goals

Others: 21 (3) games, 2 goals

Total: 254 (26) games, 16 goals

CITY HONOURS:

Promotion from Second Division 75/6

Anglo-Scottish Cup 77/8

OTHER CLUBS:

West Bromwich Albion 81/2-86/7 (168, 6)

Wolverhampton Wanderers on loan 86/7 (2, 0)

Portsmouth 87/8-88/9 (65, 2)

Exeter City 89/90-90/1 (46, 5)

CLIVE WHITEHEAD

1973/74 — 1981/82

CLIVE WHITEHEAD was one of the most exciting young wingers in the country, and Bristol City turned him into a full-back. Such a bald summation may appear to lack sympathy with manager Alan Dicks's valiant four-year struggle to sustain the club as a First Division force, but the fact remains that an entertainer of untold potential was converted into a competent defender – and the Robins went down anyway.

The curly-haired flankman's early outings left little doubt that Dicks had unearthed Ashton Gate's most skilful player since Jantzen Derrick. Unfortunately, like his predecessor, Clive could captivate one minute and exasperate the next. At his best he was sensational; sidling up to opponents with an ungainly, almost knock-kneed gait which belied his explosive intentions, he would accelerate suddenly, striding past them with the ball seemingly grafted on to his left foot, before crossing it at speed.

After an enterprising contribution on the run-in to promotion from the Second Division in 1975/76 – one of his goals, which were almost in the blue-moon category, beat Portsmouth to clinch a place in the top flight – Clive struck brilliant form among the elite. In the opener at Highbury, his control and change of pace frequently confounded one of Britain's most accomplished rearguards, and it was from his precise cross that Paul Cheesley headed the game's only goal. His progress continued with a series of thrilling performances, admittedly interspersed with some frustrating ones, and the booking rate among full-backs soared as they resorted to violence to stop him.

But the gifted Brummie found consistency difficult to acquire, and, when left-sided attacker Gert Meijer arrived in the spring of 1979, Clive was handed the number-three shirt. He proved to be an accomplished defender, his speed and strength standing him in good stead, and at times he was dangerous on the overlap. Over the next two terms, as the troubled Robins slid through the Second and into the Third Division, Clive filled various roles, including his original one and centre-back.

However, a player of his class clearly needed a higher grade of football, and when West Bromwich Albion stepped in with a £100,000 bid he tore up his 11-year contract – the longest in the League's history – and headed for the Hawthorns. Clive went on to enjoy a creditable career at the back, but the feeling will always persist among lovers of adventurous wing play that a prodigious talent went to waste.

BORN: Bristol, 17.2.40

CITY RECORD:

League: 187 games, 76 goals

FA Cup: 19 games, 5 goals

League Cup: 6 games, 0 goals

Others: 2 games, 1 goal

Total: 214 games, 82 goals

CITY HONOURS:

Promotion from Third Division 64/5

OTHER CLUBS:

Rotherham United 64/5-66/7 (47, 12)

Bristol Rovers 66/7-68/9 (29, 5)

Reading 69/70-70/1 (64, 20)

BOBBY WILLIAMS

BOBBY WILLIAMS was an extraordinary Third Division footballer. Operating at inside-left he was the closest thing Bristol City had to a schemer, yet he scored 60 League goals in his last three full seasons at Ashton Gate. It was hardly surprising that his sale to Rotherham United for £9,200 in February 1965 provoked widespread astonishment, even outrage in some quarters, on the Ashton Gate terraces.

Admittedly, the slim, elusive Bristolian, dubbed 'Shadow' for his knack of ghosting unnoticed into dangerous positions, had been ousted from the side by Gerry Sharpe before the transfer, and at the time the Yorkshire-men's cheque may have seemed a handsome one for a reserve player. But in view of the Robins' Second Division aspirations – indeed, they clinched promotion that very spring – the decision to part with a 25-year-old of Bobby's class and all-round ability was difficult to understand. With the experience of more than 200 senior games to draw on he must surely have been a major asset in the higher grade, where his delicate touch would have been at more of a premium than in the rough-and-tumble of the Third.

Supporters of the deal pointed to Bobby's relatively unsuccessful spell with Rotherham, themselves in the Second, but failed to take into account the effect the upheaval of the move may have had on his game – so many West Countrymen are bad travellers – or that he had been parted from John Atyeo and Brian Clark, fellow members of a devastatingly effective City inside trio.

Though sometimes easily dispossessed and hardly a fearsome tackler, Bobby was quick, skilful and neat, adept at delivering perfectly weighted passes and creating space for colleagues by making perceptive runs off the ball. As well as enjoying such a productive understanding with the two big strikers, he linked well with mercurial winger Jantzen Derrick, and often he was the creative fulcrum of the City attack.

Despite all his prompting activities, Bobby found time to score heavily himself. He didn't have a strong shot, but so often a goalkeeper would make a fine save from John or Brian, only to see 'Shadow' materialise in front of him to slide home the rebound.

After his brief stay in the north, Bobby dismayed City fans by joining Rovers, but he didn't suit the Eastville style and soon moved on to Reading, where he became a coach.

BORN: Bristol, 17.11.21

DIED: 1.80

CITY RECORD:

League: 296 games, 69 goals

FA Cup: 22 games, 9 goals

Total: 318 games, 78 goals

CITY HONOURS:

Third Division South Championship 54/5

OTHER CLUBS:

West Bromwich Albion 48/9-50/1 (71, 19)

CYRIL WILLIAMS

1945/46 — 1947/48 & 1951/52 — 1957/58

THERE WAS THUNDEROUS WRATH among Bristol City fans when Cyril Williams, a ball-playing schemer of silken skills, was transferred to West Bromwich Albion in the summer of 1948. It wasn't even as if the Robins were making a fortune from the deal. All they received in exchange for one of their chief entertainers, the creative force behind a team that had ridden high in the Third Division South for two successive seasons, was £500 and Cliff Edwards, a rather mundane wing-half.

Cyril, on the other hand, was anything but mundane. When he was on song he was as subtle a practitioner of the footballing art as might be found anywhere outside the top flight. 'Twinkletoes', as he was known to Ashton Gate regulars, could torment opponents with a bewitching dribble, tackle briskly for one of such slight stature, and pop up with a goal at the most opportune of moments. But what made him special was his talent for passing imaginatively, accurately and with perfectly-judged weight. Cyril was at his most dangerous when a long ball from a City defender sailed over his head and was nodded back to him by his centre-forward. If the striker turned and sprinted into space he could almost guarantee that when he glanced down, there at his side would be the ball, delivered with precision by a consummate artist.

Luckily for the Robins, after helping Albion reach the First Division, Cyril couldn't settle in the Midlands and returned to his first club for £4,500 in 1951. Though by then nearly 30, he was very fit, and was still a crucial influence when City took the title in 1954/55.

A humorous, quick-witted individual on the field and off it, Cyril proved himself too sharp for a referee in one Yuletide clash at Aldershot. The official had just sent off City 'keeper Frank Clack for his part in a fracas that had little to do with seasonal goodwill when Cyril ran the length of the pitch to plead 'You can't do that on Christmas Day!' The referee changed his mind, and the visitors went home with a point that would otherwise surely have been lost.

Cyril, the father-in-law of City's 1960s full-back Alec Briggs, played in three Second Division campaigns before retiring in 1958. A successful business career was cut tragically short when he was killed in a road accident in 1980, but his reputation as one of the most gifted of post-war Robins lives on. Had it not been for the conflict, which delayed his senior breakthrough by six seasons, Cyril might have achieved even more.

BORN: South Shields, Co. Durham, 23.3.38

CITY RECORD:

League: 146 (3) games, 9 goals

FA Cup: 8 games, 0 goals

League Cup: 11 games, 1 goal

Total: 165 games, 10 goals

OTHER CLUBS:

Gateshead 58/9-59/60 (7, 0)

Southampton 61/2-67/8 (152, 9)

KEN WIMSHURST

1967/68 — 1971/72

IF A CARICATURIST were to commit the image of Ken Wimshurst to paper, he might portray the cultured right-half taking the field in a pin-striped suit and bowler hat, a rolled umbrella over his arm. Ken was immaculate in everything he did, his game as polished and neat as his appearance, and he exuded class from the moment he checked in at Ashton Gate as new manager Alan Dicks's first signing in October 1967. The £15,000 capture from Southampton, who had played a major part in establishing the Saints as a First Division force, was just the sort of influence Bristol City needed if they were to think in terms of reaching the big time themselves.

Ken, never the most rapid of movers, was now approaching 30 and a little on the pedestrian side for the top flight, but as for his distribution, control and vision, well, that was another story. Throughout the 1960s and 1970s, it is doubtful whether the Robins boasted a more precise passer of the ball than this most composed of creators, who was initially drafted into the team in place of former skipper Gordon Low.

The thoughtful north-easterner, who had spells with Newcastle United and Wolves without playing a senior game for either before his successful six-year sojourn at The Dell, was a reassuring sight as he sallied smoothly out of the City half. He radiated confidence, but there were times when his fluent service was to little avail because colleagues were not experienced enough to read his intentions. One man who did relish linking up with Ken was right-winger Alan Skirton, who had also sampled life among the elite, and together they constructed some of the struggling Robins' most attractive and dangerous moves.

In 1971/72 Ken enjoyed an accomplished stint at right-back in an improving side that was at last beginning to look a little more like First Division candidates than relegation fodder, and then retired. He went on to succeed John Sillett as first-team coach, and when Alan Dicks was sacked in 1980 he spent three weeks as joint caretaker-boss with assistant manager Tony Collins. Later Ken coached a leading Egyptian club before returning to Bristol to run a shop and then take another job outside the game. He reverted to football to take charge of Southampton's School of Excellence in Bath, and his young charges could hardly have asked for a more impeccable example of skill and professionalism.

On the Bench

MARK AIZLEWOOD
1990/91 – 1993/94
115 (4) games, 3 goals

DANNY BARTLEY
1965/66 – 1972/73
99 (8) games, 7 goals

TERRY BUSH
1960/1 – 1969/70
166 (16) games, 45 goals

BOB ANDERSON
1954/55 – 1958/59
112 games, 0 goals

STEVE BROOKER
2004/05 –
34 games, 16 goals

TOM CASEY
1958/59 – 1962/63
133 games, 9 goals

JOHN BAILEY
1988/89 – 1990/91
103 (1) games, 1 goal

AARON BROWN
1998/99 – 2003/04
160 (32) games, 12 goals

DANNY COLES
2000/01 – 2004/05
172 (8) games, 8 goals

DARREN BARNARD
1995/96 – 1996/97
93 (1) games, 17 goals

MATT BRYANT
1990/91 – 1995/96
230 (3) games, 7 goals

TERRY COOPER
1978/79 & 1982/83 – 1984/85
56 (29) games, 1 goal

PETER CORMACK
1976/77 – 1979/80
65 (10) games, 16 goals

JOHN EMANUEL
1971/72 – 1975/76
134 (6) games, 10 goals

MATT HEWLETT
1993/94 – 1999/2000
132 (21) games, 12 goals

CHRIS CROWE
1966/67 – 1968/69
77 (1) games, 16 goals

TONY FITZPATRICK
1979/80 – 1980/81
98 games, 1 goal

MATT HILL
1998/99 – 2004/05
224 (22) games, 6 goals

KEITH CURLE
1983/84 – 1987/88
144 (9) games, 1 goal

TONY FORD
1961/62 – 1969/70
185 (1) games, 12 goals

WALLY HINSHELWOOD
1955/56 – 1959/60
158 games, 19 goals

ROB EDWARDS
1991/92 – 1998/99
229 (34) games, 8 goals

GREG GOODRIDGE
1996/97 – 2001/02
94 (54) games, 17 goals

BOBBY HUTCHINSON
1984/85 – 1986/87
115 (3) games, 13 goals

TREVOR JACOBS
1966/67 – 1972/73
145 (1) games, 3 goals

STEVE NEVILLE
1984/85 – 1987/88
156 (9) games, 49 goals

HOWARD PRITCHARD
77/78 – 80/81 & 83/84 – 85/86
185 (13) games, 31 goals

BOBBY KELLARD
1968/69 – 1969/70
84 games, 8 goals

GARY OWERS
1994/95 – 1997/98
148 (5) games, 12 goals

DAVID RENNIE
1989/90 – 1991/92
123 (3) games, 8 goals

CLIFF MORGAN
1931/32 – 1948/49
271 games, 9 goals

LEE PEACOCK
2000/01 – 2003/04
162 (13) games, 63 goals

DICKIE ROOKS
1969/70 – 1971/72
110 games, 5 goals

DAVID MOYES
1985/86 – 1987/88
109 games, 10 goals

ROGER 'LOU' PETERS
1960/61 – 1967/68
176 games, 27 goals

MARK SHAIL
1992/93 – 1999/2000
137 (12) games, 5 goals

GARY SHELTON
1989/90 – 1993/94
179 (1) games, 27 goals

ALEX TAIT
1960/61 – 1963/64
134 games, 44 goals

KEITH WAUGH
1984/85 – 1988/89
221 games, 0 goals

DAVID SMITH
1989/90 – 1991/92
112 (5) games, 14 goals

TONY THORPE
1998/99 – 2001/02
122 (29) games, 61 goals

KEITH WELCH
1991/92 – 1998/99
318 games, 0 goals

PETER SPIRING
1969/70 – 1972/73
65 (7) games, 17 goals

BERT TINDILL
1957/58 – 1958/59
59 games, 31 goals

LUKE WILKSHIRE
2003/04 –
80 (6) games, 13 goals

PAUL STEVENS
1977/78 – 1984/85
177 (1) games, 3 goals

JOHNNY WATKINS
1953/54 – 1958/59
103 games, 21 goals

ALAN WILLIAMS
1956/57 – 1960/61
145 games, 2 goals

In the Dug-Out

Bob Hewison 1932 – 1949

Bob Wright 1949 – 1950

Pat Beasley 1950 – 1958

Peter Doherty 1958 – 1960

Fred Ford 1960 – 1967

Alan Dicks 1967 – 1980

Bobby Houghton 1980 – 1982

Roy Hodgson 1982

Terry Cooper 1982 – 1988

Joe Jordan 1988 – 1990

Jimmy Lumsden 1990 – 1992

Denis Smith 1992 – 1993

Russell Osman 1993 – 1994

Joe Jordan 1994 – 1997

John Ward 1997 – 1998

Benny Lennartsson 1998 – 1999

Tony Pulis 1999

Tony Fawthrop 2000

Danny Wilson 2000 – 2004

Brian Tinnion 2004 –

Fred Ford

Alan Dicks

Danny Wilson

THE WINNING FANS

The **Bristol Evening Post** offered its readers a unique chance to get involved with this second edition of **Bristol City Greats**.

The newspaper, which supplied many of the photographs in the book, invited Bristol football fans to nominate the one player they reckoned was most deserving of a place in our updated hall of fame.

The idea was to find out who was the most popular Robin of the last 15 years, and the people who matter the most have voted overwhelmingly for current Ashton Gate boss Brian Tinnion.

The supporter who gave the best reason for his or her selection, in no more than 20 words, was promised inclusion in the book, together with a free copy of the publication.

The winner is **Daniel Holbrook** of Filton, who wrote: 'Brian's been a good player for many years, never let the team down, and is just as effective as manager.'

Runners-up, who also receive **Bristol City Greats**, are **John Lewis** of Fishponds, **Dennis Franklin** of Wraxall and **Becky Cottrell** of Keynsham.